Cambridge IGCSE®
ICT
STUDY AND REVISION GUIDE

Graham Brown
David Watson

HODDER
EDUCATION
AN HACHETTE UK COMPANY

The Publishers would like to thank the following for permission to reproduce copyright material.

Photo credits

p.1 *l* © © Shaffandi/123RF, *r* © Mikekiev/123RF; **p.6** © Ing. Richard Hilber/https://commons.wikimedia.org/wiki/File:Inside_Z9_2094.jpg; **p.7** *l* © Aimage/123RF, *r* © Nataliya Hora/123RF; **p.11** *l* © Lucian Milasan/123RF, *r* © Sittinon Supawanit/123RF; **p.18** *l* © Amnach kinchokawat/123RF, *r* © Vadim Ermak/123RF; **p.25** *l* © Aleksanderdn/123RF, r © Anatol Adutskevich/123RF; p.29 © Ohmega1982/Shutterstock.com; **p.41** © Maksym yemelyanov/123RF; p.48 l © Marco Saracco/123RF, r © Yuriy Klochan/123RF; **p.49** *l* © Mariusz Blach/123RF, *r* © Yuri Maryunin/123RF; **p.50** © Artpartner.de/Alamy Stock Photo; **p.55** © Rostislav Sedláček/123RF; **p.57** © Piero Cruciatti/Alamy Stock Photo; **p.60** *l* © Tyler Olson /123RF, *r* © Wojciech kaczkowski/123RF; **p.80** *t* © Pixelrobot/123RF, c © Bkilzer/123RF, b © Galina Peshkova/123RF; **p.81** *t* © Franck Boston/123RF, *b* © Alexutemov/123RF; **p.87** *l* © Ion Chiosea/123RF, *r* © Dzianis Rakhuba/123RF; **p.91** *l* © Supreeth Bhat/123RF, *r* © Aniwhite/123RF; **p.101** © Mike Pellinni/Shutterstock.com; **p.131** *l* © Regular/Shutterstock.com, *r* © Matej Kastelic/Shutterstock.com.

t = top, *b* = bottom, *c* = centre, *l* = left, *r* = right

Acknowledgements

Every effort has been made to trace all copyright holders, but if any have been inadvertently overlooked, the Publishers will be pleased to make the necessary arrangements at the first opportunity.

Although every effort has been made to ensure that website addresses are correct at time of going to press, Hodder Education cannot be held responsible for the content of any website mentioned in this book. It is sometimes possible to find a relocated web page by typing in the address of the home page for a website in the URL window of your browser.

® IGCSE is the registered trademark of Cambridge International Examinations. The questions, example answers, marks awarded and/or comments that appear in this book were written by the authors. In an examination, the way marks would be awarded to answers like these may be different. This book has not been through the Cambridge endorsement process.

Hachette UK's policy is to use papers that are natural, renewable and recyclable products and made from wood grown in sustainable forests. The logging and manufacturing processes are expected to conform to the environmental regulations of the country of origin.

Orders: please contact Bookpoint Ltd, 130 Milton Park, Abingdon, Oxon OX14 4SB. Telephone: (44) 01235 827720. Fax: (44) 01235 400454. Email education@bookpoint.co.uk Lines are open from 9 a.m. to 5 p.m., Monday to Saturday, with a 24-hour message answering service. You can also order through our website: www.hoddereducation.com

ISBN: 9781471890338

© Graham Brown and David Watson 2017

First published in 2017 by
Hodder Education,
An Hachette UK Company
Carmelite House
50 Victoria Embankment
London EC4Y 0DZ

www.hoddereducation.com

Impression number   10 9 8 7 6 5 4 3 2 1

Year   2021 2020 2019 2018 2017

Cover photo © Oleksiy Mark – Fotolia

Illustrations by Aptara Inc.

Typeset in India by Aptara Inc.

Printed in Spain

A catalogue record for this title is available from the British Library.

Contents

REVISED

Introduction

Welcome to the Cambridge IGCSE® ICT Study and Revision Guide. This book has been written to help you prepare fully for your ICT Examination. Following the ICT syllabus, it covers all the key content as well as sample questions and answers and practice questions to help you check your understanding and to learn the key points for gaining the best examination grade of which you are capable.

How to use this book

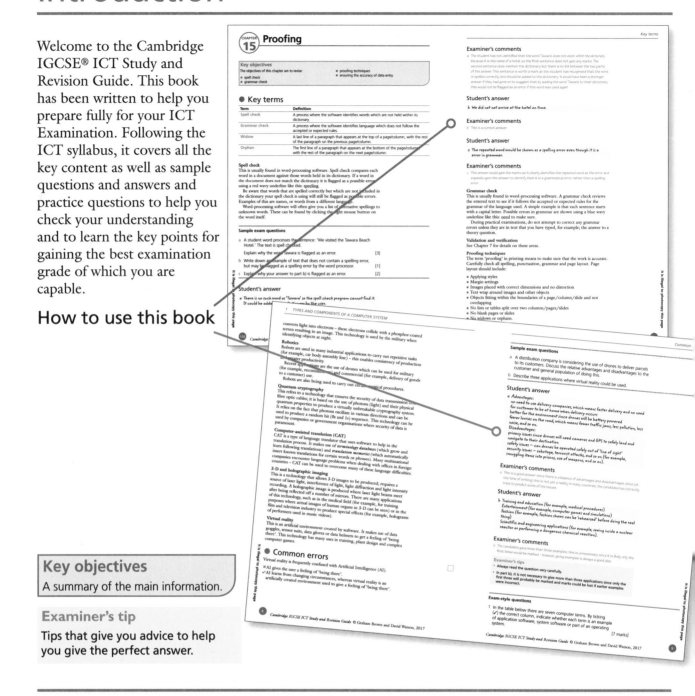

Key objectives
A summary of the main information.

Examiner's tip
Tips that give you advice to help you give the perfect answer.

Sample exam questions

Exam-style questions for you to think about.

Student's answers

Model student answers to see how the question might be answered.

Examiner's comments

Feedback from an examiner showing what was good and what could be improved.

Exam-style questions

Exam questions for you to try to see what you have learned.

CHAPTER 1

Types and components of a computer system

Key objectives
The objectives of this chapter are to revise:
- software
- hardware
- main components of a computer system
- operating systems
- different types of computer system
- emerging technologies.

● Key terms

Term	Definition
Application software	Programs that allow the user to do specific tasks on a computer.
System software	Programs that allow the hardware to run properly and allow the user to communicate with the computer.
CPU	Central Processing Unit. The part of a computer that interprets and executes commands from computer hardware and software.
Microprocessor	Single integrated circuit which is at the heart of most computers; incorporates the functions of a CPU on a single circuit board.
Operating system	Software running in the background of a computer; it manages many functions, such as user interface, error handling, memory management and managing user accounts.

● Software and hardware

Hardware consists of all the physical components of a computer system, while software refers to the programs used for controlling the operation of a computer or for processing electronic data.

Figure 1.1 Examples of hardware and software

Application software

Software that is designed so a user can perform a specific function on a computer is known as application software. With this software a user is able to browse the internet, watch a video, write an email, and much more.

Word processor

This is used to manipulate text documents and text entered via a keyboard; the software has such features as editing, saving and manipulating text; copy and paste; spell checker and thesaurus; importing photos, text and spreadsheets; translation of text into other languages.

Spreadsheet
Used to organise and manipulate numerical data; data is organised in cells in a grid of lettered columns and numbered rows; common features include: formulae to carry out calculations; ability to produce graphs; data replication; ability to do modelling and 'what if' scenarios.

Database
Used to organise, manipulate and analyse data; uses one or two tables to organise the data; tables are made up of records; common functions include ability to carry out queries on data and produce reports, and add, delete and modify data in tables.

Control/measuring
Designed to allow computer/microprocessor to interface with sensors to allow: physical quantities in the real world to be measured; control of processes by comparing sensor data with pre-stored data and sending out signals to alter process parameters (for example, open/close a valve).

Apps
Type of software that usually runs on tablets or mobile phones; examples include music streaming, GPS and camera facility (but there are thousands of Apps available).

Photo editing
Allows user to manipulate digital photos, for example change the brightness, contrast, colour saturation, remove 'red eye', and so on.

Video editing
Allows user to manipulate videos, for example, addition of titles, colour correction, creating transitions between video clips, and so on.

Graphics manipulation
Allows bit map and vector images to be changed; allows the manipulation of lines, curves and text depending on the format of the original image.

Systems software

Compiler
A program that translates high-level language code into machine code so that it can be run on a computer (that is, it produces *object code* from original *source code*).

Interpreter
This is software that directly executes a program without previously compiling it into a machine language.

Linker
A program that takes one or more object files (modules) produced by a compiler and combines them into a single program that can be run on a computer.

Operating system (OS)
Software running in the background of a computer; it manages many functions such as user interface, error handling, memory management and managing user accounts.

Device driver
Software that enables one or more hardware devices to communicate with a computer's operating system; as soon as a device is plugged in, the operating system looks for the correct device driver.

Cambridge IGCSE ICT Study and Revision Guide © Graham Brown and David Watson, 2017

Utilities
Software designed to carry out specific tasks on a computer, such as anti-virus, anti-spyware, file management and disk defragmenter.

Internal computer hardware

Motherboard
A printed circuit board that allows the processor and other computer hardware to function and communicate with each other; acts as a 'hub' that other computer devices connect to.

RAM
Random Access Memory; an internal chip where data is temporarily stored (data is lost on switching off the computer, which gives it the name *volatile memory*); RAM can be read from or written to and stores the data or part of the operating system currently in use.

ROM
Read Only Memory; memory used to store data that needs to be permanent (data is kept even when the computer is switched off, which gives it the name *non-volatile memory*); data on the ROM cannot be altered or deleted, which is why it is used to store computer configuration or the BIOS.

Video card
Allows the computer to send graphical data to a video display device such as a monitor, television or projector; it is made up of a processor, RAM, cooling mechanism/heat sink and connections.

Sound card
An integrated circuit board that provides the computer with the ability to produce sound via speakers or headphones; uses FM synthesis or wavetable synthesis to translate digital data into analogue data (to drive the speakers/headphones).

HDD/SSD
Hard disk drive and solid state drive; devices built into a computer to allow data to be stored for later use or to store application software, photos, videos and more; SSD is a more modern system with no moving parts, whereas HDD uses rotating magnetised platters and read/write heads.

CPU
Central processing unit; part of the computer that interprets and executes commands from computer hardware and software; usually part of the motherboard.

Microprocessor
The CPU is often referred to as a microprocessor; it is a single integrated circuit made up of the control unit, arithmetic-logic unit (ALU) and RAM.

Operating systems
One program manages the hardware and software of a computer, and makes it possible for programs to function; it is known as the operating system.

Command line interface
In a CLI, the user interfaces with the computer by typing in commands; the syntax of each command must be exactly correct – thus it can be a slow, error-prone process; however, the user is in direct communication with the computer and not restricted to some pre-determined options.

Cambridge IGCSE ICT Study and Revision Guide © Graham Brown and David Watson, 2017

Graphical user interface

In a GUI, the user interacts using a pointing device (such as a mouse) and icons on a computer screen; clicking on an icon launches an App; GUI is often part of a WIMP (windows, icon, menu and pointing) environment; the user doesn't have to learn any commands and it is, therefore, easier/quicker for a novice to use.

● Common errors

It is very common to see confusion between RAM and ROM; it is important to know the key differences between these two types of primary memory.

* ✖ ROM is memory used to store data temporarily, such as the data or part of the operating system currently in use.
* ✔ RAM is memory used to store data temporarily; ROM stores data permanently, and this data cannot be altered or deleted.

It is also common to see the following three terms confused: linkers, compilers and interpreters. For example:

* ✖ A linker translates a program into machine code.
* ✔ A compiler converts a program written in high-level code into machine code; compilers use programs called linkers which use some of the object files (modules) produced by a compiler and combine them into a single program that can then be run on a computer.

Sample exam questions

a   Name three examples of application software and give a feature of each.

b   Explain the function of the following:

   i   motherboard

   ii   video card

   iii   sound card.

Student's answer

a   Control software: measures physical quantities from real world using sensors; controls a process by comparing sensor readings with pre-stored data and sends out signals to, for example, open or close a valve.
   Database: organising, manipulating and analysing of data; made up of tables containing records; allows queries and reports to be produced.
   Photo editing software: allows manipulation of digital photos; can change brightness, contrast, remove 'red eye', and so on.

Examiner's comments

a   The candidate has wisely chosen three very different examples of application software. Only one feature was asked for in the question, but the candidate has given examples as well as features – this is always a wise precaution in case the chosen feature is inadequate or vague in its description.

Cambridge IGCSE ICT Study and Revision Guide © Graham Brown and David Watson, 2017

Student's answer

b i Motherboard: allows processor and other computer hardware to function and communicate with each other; acts as a 'hub' that other computer devices connect to.
  ii Video card: allows a computer to send graphical data to a video display unit such as a monitor, TV or projector.
  iii Sound card: provides a computer with the ability to produce sound via a speaker or headphones; uses FM or wavelength synthesis to translate digital data into analogue data to drive the speakers.

Examiner's comments

b The candidate has given more than would be needed to gain the full marks; the question only asks for the function so it is a little vague about how much detail is actually required.

Examiner's tip

To determine the depth of answer required, always look at the mark allocation and the space given to write the answer. Try not to exceed the amount of space allocated. If you do make a mistake or need more space, be very careful to indicate to the examiner where the rest of your answer is written. Most papers are now marked online, so examiners only see the page where your answer is written unless you guide them to another page.

● Types of computer

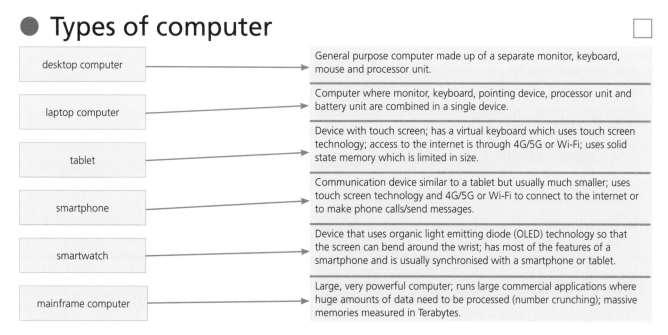

desktop computer	General purpose computer made up of a separate monitor, keyboard, mouse and processor unit.
laptop computer	Computer where monitor, keyboard, pointing device, processor unit and battery unit are combined in a single device.
tablet	Device with touch screen; has a virtual keyboard which uses touch screen technology; access to the internet is through 4G/5G or Wi-Fi; uses solid state memory which is limited in size.
smartphone	Communication device similar to a tablet but usually much smaller; uses touch screen technology and 4G/5G or Wi-Fi to connect to the internet or to make phone calls/send messages.
smartwatch	Device that uses organic light emitting diode (OLED) technology so that the screen can bend around the wrist; has most of the features of a smartphone and is usually synchronised with a smartphone or tablet.
mainframe computer	Large, very powerful computer; runs large commercial applications where huge amounts of data need to be processed (number crunching); massive memories measured in Terabytes.

Some advantages and disadvantages of computer types.

Computer	Advantages	Disadvantages
Desktop	• have better specification (for example, faster processor) for given price than the others • since not portable, less likely to be damaged/stolen • more stable internet connection since it is often hard-wired	• not portable due to separate components being used • because they aren't portable, it is necessary to copy data/files on to memory sticks or to the cloud, for example • more cumbersome due to trailing wires, desktop space
Laptop	• lightweight and self-contained, therefore portable and no trailing wires • lower power consumption than desktop • can be used anywhere if there is a Wi-Fi hotspot	• easier to break or steal since portable • limited battery life or need to carry heavy adaptor • keyboards and pointing devices can be awkward to use

Computer	Advantages	Disadvantages
Tablet	• very fast 'power up' • fully portable; small and light • no need for input devices since uses touch screen and Apps • uses solid state devices; therefore, produces little heat	• limited memory • typing on a touch screen can be very slow and error-prone • transfer of files can be a slow process • need to use an App store for most software
Smartphone/watch	• always on your person since it is small and lightweight • can make phone calls as well as 'surf' the net • can be used anywhere since uses Wi-Fi and 4G/5G • battery life is much longer than laptops	• small screen makes pages difficult to read • small keyboard makes data entry slow and error-prone • Apps, such as camera App, can drain battery quickly • small memory size • not all website features can be displayed • slow data transfer

Mainframe computers are still used today in spite of the massive increase in processing power and memory of desktop computers. They are recognised by their ability to carry out massive 'number crunching exercises' and to store massive amount of data.

● Common errors

✖ Unlike other devices, desktop computers require electricity to operate.
✔ All computers require electricity to operate, however while a desktop computer must be connected to a power supply directly, laptops, tablets and smartphones have built-in batteries that, once charged, allow them to be used when no power supply is available.

Sample exam questions

a Describe four features you would expect to find on tablets and smartphones.

b Choose suitable devices for each of the following applications. In each case, give a reason for your choice. You must choose a different device for each application.

   i   A reporter 'in the field' sending data back immediately to head office.

   ii A person wishing to monitor their health/exercises while 'on the go' wherever they are.

   iii A bank wishing to number-crunch a lot of data at the end of the month, for example accounts.

Student's answer

a *Sensors, such as accelerometers, to detect orientation of the device.*
Front-and back-facing cameras to allow photos/videos to be taken, but also allow video calls to be made.
Bluetooth connection to printers and other devices which allows wireless connectivity.
Sophisticated speech-recognition systems (for example, 'Siri') and security devices such as fingerprint scanning before device can be used.

Examiner's comments

a *Other features are possible; it is important that the given features are less likely to be found on laptops or desktops. The candidate has correctly expanded on their answers rather than just naming a feature.*

Cambridge IGCSE ICT Study and Revision Guide © Graham Brown and David Watson, 2017

Student's answer

b i Tablet: lightweight and can use 4G/5G or Wi-Fi to send data back to head
   office instantly; less bulky and easier to use than a laptop and also better
   battery life.
  ii Smartwatch: can wear the device on the wrist at all times gathering data
   to allow health/activity monitoring throughout the day.
  iii Mainframe computer: large amounts of data need very fast processors and
   large amounts of memory so that all the data can be processed quickly.

Examiner's comments

b i As long as the named device can be fully justified (for example, use of a smartphone
   rather than a tablet since you are more likely to have it on your person because of its
   small size and weight, and can make phone calls to head office) there is no one answer to
   the first part of this question.
  ii In the second part, a mobile phone could again be used provided it wasn't used in the first
   part.
  iii In the third part, it is unlikely that another device could be used, although it may be
   possible to justify the use of a desktop due to ever-increasing memory size and faster
   processors.

Examiner's tip

Always read the question very carefully. In part a, it is important not to give more
than four features since only the first four will be marked and marks could be lost if
earlier examples were incorrect. In part b, the question asked for *different* devices
in each given application – it is, therefore, important not to repeat your devices
otherwise marks will be lost.

● Emerging technologies

Figure 1.2 Examples of emerging technologies

Artificial Intelligence (AI) biometrics

This uses dynamic profiling, for example, the system learns by using AI each
time a person's fingers are scanned; hence it doesn't matter if the finger
is placed in exactly the right position each time. This is also true of other
biometrics and means biometric security systems are becoming increasingly
more reliable.

Vision enhancement

LVES (low-vision enhancement systems) allow images to be projected inside
a headset placed in front of the user's eyes. An example of its use includes
helping the visually impaired.

NVE (night vision enhancement) uses infrared light to enable an image to be seen in apparent darkness; it makes use of an image intensifier tube which converts light into electrons – these electrons collide with a phosphor-coated screen resulting in an image. This technology is used by the military when identifying objects at night.

Robotics
Robots are used in many industrial applications to carry out repetitive tasks (for example, car body assembly line) – this enables consistency of production and greater productivity.

Recent applications are the use of drones which can be used for military (for example, reconnaissance) and commercial (for example, delivery of goods to a customer) use.

Robots are also being used to carry out certain surgical procedures.

Quantum cryptography
This refers to a technology that ensures the security of data transmission over fibre optic cables; it is based on the use of photons (light) and their physical quantum properties to produce a virtually unbreakable cryptography system. It relies on the fact that photons oscillate in various directions and can be used to produce a random bit (0s and 1s) sequence. This technology can be used by companies or government organisations where security of data is paramount.

Computer-assisted translation (CAT)
CAT is a type of language translator that uses software to help in the translation process. It makes use of *terminology databases* (which grow and learn following translations) and *translation memories* (which automatically insert known translations for certain words or phrases). Many multinational companies encounter language problems when dealing with offices in foreign countries – CAT can be used to overcome many of these language difficulties.

3-D and holographic imaging
This is a technology that allows 3-D images to be produced; requires a source of laser light, interference of light, light diffraction and light intensity recording. A holographic image is produced where laser light beams meet after being reflected off a number of mirrors. There are many applications of this technology, such as in the medical field (for example, for training purposes where actual images of human organs in 3-D can be seen) or in the film and television industry to produce special effects (for example, holograms of performers used in music videos).

Virtual reality
This is an artificial environment created by software. It makes use of data goggles, sensor suits, data gloves or data helmets to get a feeling of 'being there'. This technology has many uses in training, plant design and complex computer games.

Common errors

Virtual reality is frequently confused with Artificial Intelligence (AI).

✖ AI gives the user a feeling of 'being there'.
✔ AI learns from changing circumstances, whereas virtual reality is an artificially created environment used to give a feeling of 'being there'.

Cambridge IGCSE ICT Study and Revision Guide © Graham Brown and David Watson, 2017

Sample exam questions

a A distribution company is considering the use of drones to deliver parcels to its customers. Discuss the relative advantages and disadvantages to the customer and general population of doing this.

b Describe three applications where virtual reality could be used.

Student's answer

a Advantages:
no need to use delivery companies, which means faster delivery and no need for customer to be at home when delivery occurs
better for the environment since drones will be battery powered
fewer lorries on the road, which means fewer traffic jams, less pollution, less noise, and so on.
Disadvantages:
privacy issues since drones will need cameras and GPS to safely land and navigate to their destination
safety issues — can drones be operated safely out of 'line of sight'
security issues — sabotage, terrorist attacks, and so on (for example, smuggling items into prisons, use of weapons, and so on).

Examiner's comments

a This is a good answer since there is a balance of advantages and disadvantages; since (at the time of writing) this is not yet a reality in many countries, the candidate has correctly tried to predict some of the issues.

Student's answer

b Training and education (for example, medical procedures)
Entertainment (for example, computer games and simulations)
Fashion (for example, fashion shows can be 'rehearsed' before doing the real thing)
Scientific and engineering applications (for example, seeing inside a nuclear reactor or performing a dangerous chemical reaction).

Examiner's comments

b The candidate gave more than three examples; this is unnecessary since it is likely only the first three would be marked – however, giving examples is always a good idea.

> **Examiner's tips**
> * Always read the question very carefully.
> * In part b, it is not necessary to give more than three applications since only the first three will probably be marked and marks could be lost if earlier examples were incorrect.

Exam-style questions

1 In the table below there are seven computer terms. By ticking (✓) the correct column, indicate whether each term is an example of application software, system software or part of an operating system. [7 marks]

Computer term	Application software	System software	Operating system
managing user accounts			
spreadsheet software			
video editing software			
error handling			
linker			
database software			
device driver			

2 a Explain the two terms: command line interface (CLI) and graphical user interface (GUI). [2 marks]

b Give **one** advantage and **one** disadvantage of using a CLI and of using a GUI. [4 marks]

3 John travels around the world to check out hotels for his travel company.

Explain the use of the following devices to help John to give his feedback and to keep in contact with his travel company back home:

laptop computer

tablet

smartwatch. [6 marks]

4 There are seven descriptions given below, on the left. In the right-hand column, write down the name of the computer term being described. [7 marks]

Description	Computer term
Uses infrared light and visible light so that an object can still be seen even when it is apparently dark	
Unmanned flying devices that can be used for army surveillance or delivering items to customers without the need for a delivery van	
System based on the fact that photons oscillate in various directions and can be used to produce a random sequence of bits when sending data over fibre optic cables	
System that uses terminology databases and translation memories to convert text written in one language into text in a different language	
Technology that uses laser light, interference of light and diffraction of light to produce a 3-D life-like image of an object	
Artificial environment that uses data goggles, sensor suits, data gloves or data helmets to create 'the feeling of being there'	
Systems used to do massive number crunching, equipped with very powerful processors and massive memories	

Input and output devices

Key objectives
The objectives of this chapter are to revise:
- the different types of common input devices, including their advantages and disadvantages
- the types of direct data entry devices
- the different types of common output devices, including their advantages and disadvantages.

● Key terms

Term	Definition
Input device	Hardware to provide data and control signals to a computer system from the outside world
Output device	Hardware that shows the results of data processing from a computer system, either in human-readable format or as control signals to another device
Pointing device	Input device that is used to control the movement of a cursor or pointer on a computer screen; used to select from menus or to launch applications
Sensor	Device that inputs data to a computer/microprocessor, usually in analogue format; the data is a measurement of some physical quantity
Direct data entry	Data entered into a computer system via an input device requiring little or no human intervention
Control applications	System using sensors and microprocessor/computer where data sent to the microprocessor/computer is compared to pre-set data; the microprocessor/computer sends out signals to control devices (for example, to switch a pump on or off) to ensure incoming data is within these pre-set data levels at all times
Measurement applications	System using sensors and microprocessor/computer, where data sent to the microprocessor/computer is compared to pre-set data; unlike a control application, the microprocessor/computer takes no action but simply warns the user that the sensor data indicates that what is being monitored is out of acceptable range (this can be a warning light, siren or output on a screen or printer)

● Input devices

Figure 2.1 Examples of input devices

Keyboard

This is the most common input device, where a user simply enters data by pressing keys; some keyboards are ergonomic in an effort to reduce the risk of RSI (repetitive strain injury) when doing a lot of typing. It is a slow and error-prone method of input but requires little or no training; keyboards can be 'virtual' when used on tablets or smartphones. Concept keyboards are often used, where icons can replace letters thus reducing the number of possible inputs. Numeric keypads are a type of keyboard where numbers and mathematical symbols only are used.

Pointing devices

These are used to control the movement of a pointer or cursor on a screen and to enable selection from a menu or to launch applications. The most common pointing devices are the mouse (including optical and wireless), touchpad (found on laptops) or trackerball (often found in control rooms or in some luxury cars to select functions such as radio or sat nav).

They are generally easier to use than a keyboard in many applications but can cause issues with people who have certain disabilities. Pointing devices tend to be used in a WIMP environment.

Remote control

Used to control the operation of certain devices wirelessly (that is, remotely); special buttons are used to operate televisions, video/CD players, air con systems, multimedia, and so on.

Joysticks

These are similar in some ways to pointing devices; a control stick is used to make movement in X-Y directions and they often have a button on the top of the stick for gaming purposes (for example, to fire a rocket).

This is related to the driving wheel which is also used in games and simulations; sensors are used to pick up the left and right movement of the steering wheel.

Touch screens

These allow the selection from a menu or the launching of applications by touching the screen in the correct place; this is done using the finger or a special conductive stylus.

Touch screens are generally much easier to use than a keyboard or mouse, but screens can get very dirty from people's fingerprints. They are often used in ATMs, mobile phones and public information systems (for example, at an airport or railway station).

Scanners

These are used to enter data/information in hard-copy (paper) format into a computer (for example, a page from a book or a photographic print). The hard-copy data is converted into an electronic form that can be stored in a computer memory.

Scanners allow old/valuable books to be stored for future use or allow documents to be pasted into an electronic document; damaged photos and pages can be restored/recovered using this method.

Digital cameras

These have largely replaced traditional film-based cameras; the image is stored on a solid state memory card and can be transferred to a computer/printer using a USB cable, Bluetooth or by inserting the memory card directly into the device.

The quality of the photos is now comparable to the best film-based cameras; they have the distinct advantage that unwanted photos can easily be deleted without the need to pay for any film developing.

Digital video cameras 'stitch' together a number of still photos; dedicated video cameras exist or ordinary digital cameras can be used to take video footage (although the quality is rarely as good as from a dedicated video camera). When using an ordinary digital camera to make videos, another drawback is the amount of memory used. Most smartphones also have a camera facility but they rarely have many of the desirable features found on a dedicated camera.

Cambridge IGCSE ICT Study and Revision Guide © Graham Brown and David Watson, 2017

Webcams

These connect directly to the computer and don't save the images; data is transmitted directly to the computer for use in video conferencing or in video calls; the quality varies a lot depending on the lens and electronics.

Microphones

These are used to convert sound into electrical signals which, once converted to digital, can be stored on a computer. Used in voice/speech recognition systems, for creating voiceovers in videos/presentations, and so on.

Graphics tablets

These are used with a stylus to produce freehand drawings which can be input into a computer and stored for later use, for example, computer-aided design (CAD) work. They are useful where artistic skills are needed, for example, in creating cartoon characters, logos, and so on.

Light pens

This technology works with cathode ray tube (CRT) screens only; it allows menu selection, moving items by dragging them across the screen with the pen and drawing directly on the screen using the pen. Light pens only work at the moment with CRT screens, but touch screens now work with a conductive stylus and allow similar actions to be done.

Sensors

These are devices that input physical analogue quantities into a computer (for example, pH values, temperatures, moisture levels, and so on). An ADC (analogue to digital converter) is usually required so that data is produced which can be understood by the computer.

● Common errors

It is very common to see students make incorrect claims about webcams.

✖ Webcams store images which are later transmitted.
✔ Webcams capture images which are then sent to the computer directly; these images are then transmitted directly during a video chat, for example.

It is also common to see students making incorrect claims about sensors.

✖ Devices such as switches and valves are switched off and on by the sensors.
✔ Sensors gather data which is constantly relayed back to a computer. After analysing this data the computer will determine whether to open or close a valve or switch.

Sample exam questions

a Compare the use of a mouse and a touch screen as a form of input.

b Discuss the advantages and disadvantages of using a keyboard as an input device.

Student's answer

a Mouse: cursor or pointer on a screen is controlled by moving the mouse; selections are made by moving the pointer over an icon and then clicking right mouse button; scroll down buttons are used to move top to bottom to make editing faster.
Touch screen: by simply touching an icon on the screen it is selected or an application is launched; touch screens can be used with a conductive stylus.

Examiner's comments

Student's answer

b Advantages: novices find a keyboard easier to use without any training; it is the standard input device and is universally used; good for word processing and entering data into spreadsheets.
Disadvantages: slow and error-prone data entry method; take up a lot of desk space where space is limited; can lead to conditions such as RSI if used a lot. Concept keyboards are used if allowed inputs are limited. RSI issues can be partially reduced by using ergonomic keyboards. Keyboards make it easy to verify input since the input is shown directly on a screen. While slow and error-prone, the keyboard continues to be one of the easiest input devices for people to use.

Examiner's comments

Examiner's tips

- The depth of answer required needs a review of the mark allocation; if the question is worth 2 marks only, then don't try and write several lines of explanation as this will be a waste of time. But if the question carries 6 marks, for example, then a much more in-depth answer would be required. Basically, read the question and look at the possible marks and the space provided before starting to compose your answer.

- In discussion or comparison questions, it is normally necessary to consider the pros and cons to make a balanced argument. It is always worth trying to come to some conclusion – but it must be based on your discussion points to have any validity.

● Direct data entry

Direct data entry (DDE) usually refers to entering data into a computer with minimal or no human intervention; thus eliminating errors, speeding up the data entry process and, in many cases, automating the data entry process. The most common examples of DDE include:

- magnetic stripe readers and chip and PIN readers
- contactless card readers

- RFID readers
- MICR
- OMR
- OCR
- barcode readers
- QR readers.

Magnetic stripe readers, and chip and PIN readers

These readers either read the magnetic stripe on the back of a card or scan the chip embedded on the front of the card. Magnetic stripes contain the account number, sort code, expiry date and start date, for example. However, a chip would contain additional information such as the PIN (these are known as EMV cards). As a data processor, the chip uses cryptography which makes it much safer than magnetic stripe technology.

It is also true that, unlike a magnetic stripe, the chip and PIN system doesn't need to be connected to a phone or the internet to process a payment; with chip and PIN, terminals can work offline using the chip only and then authorise charges in bulk at the end of the day. Remember, however, that chip and PIN doesn't use radio frequency identification (RFID) technology. Both magnetic stripe and chip and PIN systems are used at ATMs or for making shop/restaurant purchases, with data captured automatically from either stripe or chip.

Contactless card readers

Contactless card payment allows payments of up to $50 at each transaction (although this limit will vary from country to country) without the need to key in a PIN. The cards have a small chip that emits radio waves and only works within a few metres of the terminal. The transaction is much faster than other methods and also uses 128-bit encryption which makes it safe – a unique number is generated for each transaction.

Radio frequency identification readers

Radio frequency identification (RFID) systems use radio waves to read and capture information stored on a tag, which can be read from several metres away. The tag is made up of a microchip (to store and process data) and an antenna (to receive/transmit data). They can be *passive* (use readers' radio wave energy) or battery powered (using a small embedded battery). They are used, for example, in the tracking of items (for example, livestock on a farm), admission passes (security device) or in libraries (to track book loans).

The RFID tag is read automatically which, since there is no need to physically scan the tag, makes them ideal for the applications mentioned above.

Magnetic ink character recognition/reader

Magnetic ink character recognition/reader (MICR) is used to read the characters on the bottom of cheques (checks) which have been printed in iron-impregnated ink; each character is read/scanned by the reader and is converted into an electronic form which can then be interpreted by a computer. MICR characters are difficult to forge and can even be written over (for example, by somebody's signature) without affecting the reading/scanning process – this is because it is the magnetic properties that are read rather than the characters themselves. They also have the advantage that the characters are both human and machine readable. However, the system is rather expensive and limited in its applications.

Optical mark recognition/reader

Optical mark recognition/reader (OMR) reads marks written in pencil or pen in specific places on a form. Forms can be filled in using a lozenge (⬬) or a line between two points (•—•).

Cambridge IGCSE ICT Study and Revision Guide © Graham Brown and David Watson, 2017

The position of possible marks on the form is stored in the computer's memory and marks made by a person filling in the form are compared to the stored positions. OMR can be used in multiple-choice exam papers (where correct mark positions for each answer are stored, enabling automatic marking of the exam paper) or questionnaires (where position of marks corresponds to a number of possible options stored in memory – thus enabling automatic data analysis). It is a very fast and accurate data entry method but doesn't allow for expansion of answers in a questionnaire, for example.

Optical character recognition/reader

Optical character recognition/reader (OCR) scans text and converts it into a computer-readable format; it can read typed characters or handwritten characters. Although faster (and more accurate) than typing in answers, the system is slower and less accurate than OMR. Some handwriting can cause problems for OCR readers. However, OCR allows people to expand on their answers in questionnaires and the forms are much less expensive to produce and there is no need to scan in and store a template.

Barcode readers

Barcodes are a series of vertical light and dark lines of varying thickness that represent data (either numerical or alphanumerical).

ISBN 978–1–471–89033–8 Hodder

The barcode can be read by a hand-held scanner or fixed scanner (for example, at a supermarket checkout). Scanners use either red laser light or red LED light to read the barcodes. They are used mainly in supermarkets (to fetch prices of goods or for automatic stock control) or libraries (on books and library cards). It is not a foolproof system since barcodes can be forged or damaged.

Quick response codes

This is another type of more sophisticated barcode which uses a matrix of dark squares on a light background.

QR codes can hold considerably more data than standard barcodes.

QR codes are read by a camera on a tablet or smartphone and the data interpreted, for example, it could contain a website which is automatically loaded up, or advertising data such as special offers or contact details. There is no need for the user to type anything in, the processing is done automatically.

● Common errors

It is very common to see students make incorrect claims about PINs used with magnetic stripes.

✖ When using magnetic credit/debit cards, the PIN is stored on the magnetic stripe on the reverse of the card.
✔ The PIN is stored on the embedded chip in the credit/debit card; however, information such as an account number and sort code is stored on a magnetic stripe.

It is also common to see students making the following errors about barcodes:

✖ The prices of goods are stored on the barcode of the goods being scanned.
✔ Barcodes represent data which identifies the item on which the barcode is fixed. A scanner reads the barcode and sends the data to a computer. This data is then used to locate the item in the stock database; the price is located from the stock file and sent back to the checkout terminal.

 Cambridge IGCSE ICT Study and Revision Guide © Graham Brown and David Watson, 2017

Sample exam questions

a   A bank decides to use barcodes on cheques rather than magnetic ink characters. Describe the advantages and disadvantages of doing this.

b   Compare OMR and OCR as a method to collect data from questionnaires.

Student's answer

a *Barcodes would be less expensive to produce and readers/scanners would also be cheaper; barcodes are easier to forge than MICR; MICR characters are both human and machine readable; barcodes cannot be read if damaged or written over, whereas MICR characters can still be read even if written over; cheques with barcodes could be scanned or photocopied and used fraudulently; MICR characters are limited.*

Examiner's comments

a *The candidate correctly gave at least one disadvantage and one advantage of both methods. This is essential when answering questions of this type to ensure a good balance and also improves the chances of gaining good marks.*

Student's answer

b *OMR: reads filled-in lozenges or pen/pencil marks; information given is limited to questions and doesn't allow any expansion of answers; reads marks on pages and compares to stored template, therefore questionnaire choices are easily recognised and processed; needs expensive forms; however, more accurate information gathering needs more 'filling in' instructions for target group. OCR: possible to read handwriting, therefore possible to allow extension to answers on the questionnaire; poor handwriting may cause problems when reading questionnaires; it is a complex recognition system; needs fewer completion instructions than OMR; less accurate and slower than OMR.*

Examiner's comments

b *The candidate has given a fairly good answer here. They have tried to tailor the answer to the given application. It is very common to see generic answers which will gain some credit, but examiners will often look for answers which refer to the application given in the question.*

> **Examiner's tip**
>
> Where a scenario/application is given, it is essential to try and adapt your knowledge to the scenario. This will give a more relevant answer and, in many cases, increase your marks. For example, if you were asked to give the benefits of using OLED technology to make television/monitor screens and you wrote 'OLED makes uses of plastic technology', you would probably gain 1 mark. But if you wrote 'OLED uses plastic which makes the screens much lighter and also allows them to be formed into any shape, for example, curved for improved viewing or for making smartwatch screens which can wrap around the wrist', then you might gain 3 marks since you have tailored your answer to the application of TVs/monitors.

Cambridge IGCSE ICT Study and Revision Guide © Graham Brown and David Watson, 2017

● Output devices

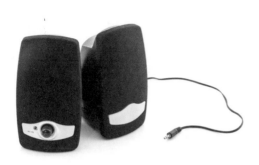

Figure 2.2 Examples of output devices

Monitors

Monitors (or screens) can be either CRT (cathode ray tube) or LCD/ LED (liquid crystal display/light emitting diode) – the latter types are often referred to as TFT (thin film transistors). LCD/LED has almost entirely replaced CRT in both the computing and commercial (television) fields. LCD screens need some form of back-lighting; this used to be CCFL (cold cathode fluorescent lamp) but now uses LED instead. The use of LEDs allowed for even thinner screens with better contrast and colour definition; they also use less electricity and don't produce as much heat. However, even this technology is now looking dated as new OLED (organic light emitting diode) screens are being developed. This allows the use of very thin plastic screens, with no need for any back-lighting, larger viewing angles and even more energy efficiency (the full list of advantages and features can be found in the Cambridge IGCSE ICT Coursebook).

Multimedia projectors

These projectors are used to project the output from a computer on to large screens or white walls. This makes them invaluable for presentations or advertising. They are referred to as multimedia since they allow for sound, animation and video as well as static displays.

Printers

The four most common printers are:

- laser
- inkjet
- dot matrix
- 3-D.

Both laser and inkjet produce high-quality outputs, but laser is better if a large number of copies needs to be printed (they have larger ink cartridges, larger buffers and much bigger paper trays – although new inkjet printers are being developed with large ink reservoirs on the side of the printer). Inkjet printers work by ejecting droplets of ink from a reservoir and build up the text/images line by line as the paper advances.

Laser printers use the properties of static electricity and use dry toner rather than liquid ink; the ink is fixed to the paper by passing it over a heated drum. This type of printer produces the whole page at once as it revolves around a printing drum. Laser printers produce ozone gas and tiny toner particulates in the air.

Dot matrix printers use older technology where a character is built up by an array of dots, for example:

Dotmatrix

Cambridge IGCSE ICT Study and Revision Guide © Graham Brown and David Watson, 2017

Dot matrix printers are noisy, poor quality and slow. However, they allow the use of continuous multi-part stationery and they are less affected by hostile atmospheres (for example, damp or dirty air).

3-D printers are the new exciting technology ready to create the next industrial revolution. These create solid objects by building them up layer by layer (using powdered resin, plastic or metal, for example) – the solid object is usually a working model. They are showing great promise in medical applications and for producing items no longer in production (for example, parts for vintage cars or invaluable museum exhibits).

Speakers

These devices convert output from a computer into sound; digital data is converted to electrical signals (using a digital to analogue converter – DAC) which drive the speakers.

Actuators

Actuators are used in control applications involving microprocessors/computers, sensors, analogue to digital convertors (ADC) and DAC. They are transducers which take signals from computers and convert them into some form of motion (for example, motor, pump, switch or valve). See Chapter 6 for more on this topic.

● Common errors

It is very common to see students confuse the operation of laser and inkjet printers.

✖ Unlike dot matrix and inkjet printers, laser printers don't use ink when producing documents.
✔ Laser printers use dry ink (called toner) unlike inkjet (which use liquid ink) and dot matrix (which use an inked ribbon).

Many candidates also make incorrect statements about dot matrix printers.

✖ Dot matrix printers are suitable for certain applications because they are noisy.
✔ Dot matrix printers are very noisy in operation; this makes them suitable for applications where noise isn't an issue, for example, on a factory floor.

Sample exam questions

a Describe the differences in televisions which use LCD/LED or OLED technology.

b An office produces designs for new toys. It is necessary to produce working models and also to give a presentation to senior managers which includes a cost breakdown and describes the development requirements. The presentation will also consider advertising of the new toys. Describe which printers would be needed by the design office, giving a reason for your choice in each case.

Student's answer

a OLED screens are thinner and lighter and are, therefore, more flexible than LCD/LED.
OLED technology is much lighter since it can use plastic layers instead of glass.
OLEDs give a brighter, more white, light than LEDs.
OLEDs don't need any back-lighting, unlike LCD screens.
OLEDs use less power and, therefore, produce less heat.
Since the layers are made of plastic, OLED screens can be made into any shape.
OLED screens have a larger field of view than LCD screens.

Examiner's comments

a The answer given probably raises more points than necessary; it would depend on the mark allocation for the question. No comparisons were made in the answer; just facts. However, there was no need to make any comparisons since the question simply asked for a description of the differences.

Student's answer

b 3-D printer — to produce working prototypes of the new toys; this will be cheaper and quicker than more conventional methods; 3-D printers also allow several prototypes to be made, making it quicker to modify toys and see the results.
Laser printer — these will be used to produce advertising brochures and leaflets; also to produce documentation and reports to hand out to the management team.

Examiner's comments

b 3-D and laser printers were the obvious choice here. Dot matrix printers would be low quality and noisy in an office; inkjets would be slow to produce a number of leaflets/brochures for handing out to potential customers/distributors. Laser printers could also be used in the production of the packaging for the toys.
However, the candidate could have suggested making photos of the toys (using an inkjet printer) or producing quality control documents/customer orders on the factory floor (where a dot matrix printer could have been suggested). As long as the choice of printer is very clear (and correct) then credit would have to be given for such answers.

Examiner's tips

- When answering questions such as part a, it is often useful to find some blank paper to jot down all your advantages/differences before putting together your final answer; this could, in the long run, save you time and help produce a more coherent response.

- Open-ended questions, such as part b, need care when considering your answer. Make sure you can justify your choice of device and you should be okay to gain the marks; but if your justification doesn't match the device, then marks will inevitably be lost.

- Take care when making comparisons. Instead of the vague, 'Laser printers are faster than inkjet printers', write a clear statement: 'Laser printers are faster at printing many pages', followed by a valid reason: 'because they have larger printer buffers and so can produce many pages faster than an inkjet printer; but for a single page the printing speed of both printers is almost the same'.

Cambridge IGCSE ICT Study and Revision Guide © Graham Brown and David Watson, 2017

Exam-style questions

1 Give the *most suitable* input device for each of the following applications.
A different device needs to be given in each case.

a Entry of data into a spreadsheet or word processor

b Selection of a menu item on a monitor by the use of a conductive stylus
or finger

c Converting the written page from a textbook into an electronic format
which can be stored on a computer

d Used in voice-recognition systems as part of security to enter a building

e Measurement of temperature in a glasshouse and sending the value to
a computer as part of a monitoring system

f Design of a freehand logo for input into a computer [6 marks]

2 a A customer pays for some items in a shop using a contactless card
payment method.

Describe the steps taken when making payment. [3 marks]

b Some of the goods in the shop are tracked using an RFID system.

i What is meant by RFID? [1 mark]

ii Name **two** of the components that make up an RFID system. [2 marks]

iii Give **two** other uses of RFID technology. [2 marks]

3 a Compare the use of OCR and OMR as a method for obtaining
and analysing data from questionnaires given out to the general
public. [4 marks]

b Copy the table. Tick (✓) the correct column to indicate the best method
of direct data entry for each of the three applications. [3 marks]

Application	MICR	Barcode reader	OMR
Reading numbers/characters on the bottom of bank cheques (checks)			
Automatically reading and marking multiple-choice question papers			
Allowing a fully automatic stock control system			

4 The following is a list of stages when text, written in magnetisable ink, is
passed over a magnetic ink character reader (MICR). The stages below are
not written in the correct order.

Copy and complete the table that follows, showing the five stages in
their correct order. [5 marks]

A As each character passes over the head it produces a unique waveform

B Characters are then passed over the MICR read head

C Ink on the paper is first magnetised

D MICR text is passed over an MICR reader

E The waveform is recognised by the computer system

Stage	Description of stage
1	
2	
3	
4	
5	

5 Many computer screens and televisions use OLED technology.

   a Give **four** advantages of using OLED technology rather than LCD/LED technology.   [4 marks]

   b Explain why CRT monitors are being phased out.   [2 marks]

6 Describe in detail the relative advantages and disadvantages of using:

laser printers

inkjet printers

dot matrix printers.   [7 marks]

Cambridge IGCSE ICT Study and Revision Guide © Graham Brown and David Watson, 2017

Storage devices and media

Key objectives

The objectives of this chapter are to revise:

- backing storage
- why we have to back up data
- the types of access used by storage devices

- the three common types of secondary storage:
  magnetic
  optical
  solid state.

Key terms

Term	Definition
Back-up data	The copying of files to a different media in case of problems with main storage; back-ups are often stored at a different location.
Serial access	How data/records are located by starting at the beginning of the file and reading through all records in order until the required one is found, for example, used on magnetic tapes.
Key field	This is a field in a record which will uniquely identify each record, for example, an account number.
Field	This is one of the pieces of data which makes up a record, for example, the date of birth in a customer's record.
Record	A group of fields which are all related to each other, for example, date of birth, address, name and account number are all fields which together make up a customer's record.
File	A group of records make up a file; these can be data files, text files, directory files, and so on.
Master file	A collection of records which contain the main data such as name, address, reference number, and so on.
Transaction file	A collection of records which are used to update a master file; these files will contain changes from a period of time, for example, new orders, new address, and so on.
Direct access	The ability to locate the required record without the need to read or scan any of the previous records, for example, used on magnetic disk.
Magnetic storage media	A system that uses magnetic properties of a coating of iron or nickel alloys to store/read data in the form of 0s and 1s.
Optical storage media	A system that uses the optical properties of laser light (blue or red) to store and read data, for example used on CDs and DVDs.
Solid state	A system that works by controlling the movement of electrons within a NAND or NOR chip; data is stored as 0s and 1s in millions of tiny transistors within the chip; most systems use NAND and are often referred to as flash memories.

Backing up of data

Data is backed up to safeguard against loss of data (for example, due to equipment failure or a malicious act). If data is lost or corrupted it can be restored using the backed-up data. Back-up files are often stored in a different location to the main storage in case of fire, for example.

Backing up of data, however, would not necessarily allow recovery following a virus infection since the virus may also have been copied during the backing-up procedure. This means when the recovered files are loaded back on to main storage, infected files may also be loaded from the back-up media.

Data stored on storage media is accessed either using serial access or direct access. Magnetic tapes use serial access, but most other back-up systems use direct access. Direct access is a considerably faster way of locating data and must be used, for example, in a real-time application (for example, booking seats on a flight).

It is illegal to photocopy this page

It is important to consider the size of files when backing up data. For example, a photograph may occupy 10 MB of storage; this means a memory stick with 4 GB capacity, for example, could store a maximum of approximately 400 photographs.

● Common errors

It is very common to see students make incorrect claims about why back-up files are made.

✖ Backing up computer files gives protection against a virus attack.
✔ Following a virus attack, backed-up files can be used to restore or recover any infected files; however, care needs to be taken to ensure that the backed-up files are not also infected with the virus – this can be done by running a virus scan on the backed-up files before they are recovered.

Sample exam questions

a   A song stored on a CD is, on average, 4 MB in size. A user wishes to transfer 8000 such songs on to a memory stick. Estimate the minimum size of memory stick, in GB, that the user will need to use.

b   Describe three ways that data could be lost from a storage device such as a hard disk drive.

Student's answer

a   *8000 × 4 ¡ 32 000 MB needed to store all 8000 songs.*
    1000 MB ¡ 1 GB
    Therefore, the user needs a minimum of 32 GB storage on the memory stick.

Examiner's comments

a   *The candidate has correctly shown all the stages in the calculation to find the size of the required memory stick.*

Student's answer

b   *Equipment failure, for example, head crash on a hard disk drive (a head crash occurs when the read/write used in the hard disk drive unit touches the surface of the disks — this can often cause damage and lead to loss of data).*
    Accidental loss of data, for example, incorrect procedure used when removing a memory stick.
    Malicious loss of data, for example, a virus or hacker deleting key exec files.

Examiner's comments

b   *Three very different situations have been described – this is important since repeating answers usually loses marks.*

Examiner's tips

*   When asked to carry out a calculation always show *all* the steps in case you make an error; credit will always be given for the method used even if the final answer is incorrect. Not showing all your steps (and just giving a final answer) could result in losing all your marks if the final answer is incorrect.

*   When asked to give more than one reason for something happening, make sure each example is significantly different to avoid repeating yourself and losing marks.

Cambridge IGCSE ICT Study and Revision Guide © Graham Brown and David Watson, 2017

● Secondary storage media

Figure 3.1 Examples of secondary storage media

Magnetic storage media

These include magnetic tape and magnetic hard disk drives (HDD). These methods rely on the magnetic properties of certain coatings (made from iron and/or nickel alloys) to allow the storage of binary data (0s and 1s).

HDD can be fixed (internal) or portable. In both cases, they use rotating disks (known as platters) which are made from glass, ceramic or aluminium coated in a magnetic material. HDDs are still a very common form of main storage on desktop computers (storage of the operating system, applications software and user's files). Portable disk drives usually connect to a computer using one of the USB connections.

Magnetic tape is an old technology that uses thin strips of plastic coated in magnetic material wound on a metal or plastic reel. The tape passes at high speed over a read/write head. They have a much slower data access time than magnetic disks, but are still used in a number of commercial applications where their massive storage capacity and reliability (long term) is very important.

Optical storage media

Optical storage is usually associated with CDs and DVDs. Laser light is used to read and write data on the surface of a polycarbonate disk. CDs and DVDs use a single spiral 'track' to store data, working from the centre to the edge.

DVDs use dual layering (that is, two recording layers sandwiched between two polycarbonate disks), which increases storage capacity when compared to CDs. They also use laser light which has a shorter wavelength than that used on CDs, which further increases their storage capacity. DVDs are used to store movies and to supply applications software. CDs are generally being phased out, but some home users still use them to store music files.

CDs and DVDs are termed 'R' (record once only) or 'RW' (allows several read and write operations). CD-Rs and DVD-Rs are used in home applications since they need less expensive read/write equipment. Often CD-Rs and DVD-Rs are *finalised,* which allows them to be used on any CD or DVD player – once finalised, a CD or DVD effectively becomes a CD-ROM or DVD-ROM since it can no longer be recorded on. There is a distinct difference in the way data is stored using home equipment and industry equipment. Home devices use a light sensitive dye on the CD/DVD surface which is used to store the 0s and 1s; industrial devices use metal alloy coatings where the data is stored as 'pits' and 'bumps'.

DVD-RAM is an old technology which is being phased out. Unlike normal DVDs, these use several concentric 'tracks' which allow simultaneous read and write operations to take place; these are being replaced by solid state memories. DVD-RAM uses similar technology to DVD-RW, with high energy lasers used to write data and low energy lasers used to read the data.

Blu-ray disks are often used instead of DVDs. Unlike DVDs, they use a blue laser source and also a single polycarbonate disk. The wavelength of blue laser light is about 40% shorter than red laser light. Consequently, they can store considerably more data than DVDs and are used to store movies and any application that requires their higher storage capacity.

Optical storage media are slowly being phased out as new technologies (such as solid state memories) become a more reliable and cheaper alternative. The longevity of data stored on optical media is still uncertain; only with time will it become clear whether or not storage on CDs or DVDS/Blu-ray is stable in the long term.

Solid state media

These have no moving parts and all data is retrieved at the same rate no matter where the data is stored on the device. They rely on the control of the movement of electrons within NAND or NOR chips. Data is stored as 0s and 1s in millions of tiny transistors within the chip. NAND technology is less expensive than NOR technology, therefore it is the type most commonly used.

When used as SSD (solid state drives) they are more reliable, thinner and lighter than HDDs. Solid state technology is also used in memory sticks/pens and in flash memory cards.

● Common errors

There is often confusion between data transfer rate and data access time.

✖ The data transfer rate for magnetic tape is very slow which is why magnetic disk drives are used.

✔ Data transfer rate is 'the speed at which data is sent from the media to the computer', whereas data access time is 'the time taken to find the data on the media'. Even systems with slow data access time (for example, magnetic tapes) can still have very fast data transfer speeds.

There is often confusion between the terms 'R' and 'ROM' when referring to CDs/DVDs.

✖ A DVD or CD using the letter 'R' indicates that it is READ ONLY.

✔ The letter 'R' indicates that it is possible to write to the CD/DVD once only; the CD/DVD only becomes a ROM once it has been 'finalised'. 'ROM' indicates that the CD/DVD can only be read from and not written to.

Sample exam questions

a Describe the main differences between DVD and Blu-ray disks for the storage of movies.

b Describe four advantages in using SSDs rather than HDDs in laptop computers.

Student's answer

a DVDs use red laser light whereas Blu-ray uses blue laser light.
The laser light used in Blu-ray disks is considerably shorter than the laser light used in DVDs.
Blu-ray uses only one polycarbonate disk whereas DVDs use a sandwich of two thinner disks.
The track pitch on Blu-ray disks is less than half the track pitch used on DVDs.
DVDs suffer from birefringence (the laser beam is split, causing reading errors due to two recording layers).

Examiner's comments

a The exact values of lasers (such as 405 nm wavelength of blue laser light or 0.3 μm track pitch) is not required at this level. It is sufficient to use 'shorter' or 'smaller' in any comparison, as the student has done.

Student's answer

b SSD is much lighter than HDD (no moving parts or disks).
SSD has a lower power consumption than HDD (this lengthens battery life on portable devices).
SSD has a lower power consumption than HDD (this produces less heat).
SSDs are very thin compared to HDDs due to no moving parts (this means laptop computers can be made very thin).

Examiner's comments

b The four advantages given were correctly specific to laptop computers. Other advantages (for example, more reliable, faster access time or 'don't need to get up to speed') are not specific to laptops and would be unlikely to gain any credit.

Examiner's tips

- Don't try and remember things like wavelength of laser light, or other such specifications – such technical knowledge would never be tested at IGCSE level.

- Part b is a good example where reading the question is so important; giving advantages relevant to laptops is key to gaining the maximum marks for this question. Answers not specific to the named application would probably lose marks since, by naming an actual application, the question is giving a strong hint about how it should be answered.

Exam-style questions

1 a Explain the difference between data transfer rate and data access time when using a secondary storage device.   [2 marks]

   b Explain the differences between DVD-R and DVD-RW.   [3 marks]

2 Which computer terms are being described below:

   a The copying of data to another media in case the original data is lost or corrupted.

   b Data/records on the media are located by starting at the beginning of the file and reading all of the records until the required one is found.

   c An item in a computer record which is used to uniquely identify each record.

   d The ability to locate a required record on a file without the need to read/scan any of the preceding records.

   e Collection of records used to update a master file, for example, change of address, new working hours for the week, and so on.   [5 marks]

3 Describe the main differences between the technology used in optical media and solid state media. You should give at least two examples of the technology used for both types of media.   [5 marks]

Cambridge IGCSE ICT Study and Revision Guide © Graham Brown and David Watson, 2017

Networks and the effects of using them

CHAPTER 4

Key objectives

The objectives of this chapter are to revise:

- networks and network devices
- IP and MAC addresses
- Wi-Fi and Bluetooth
- setting up small networks
- LAN, WAN and WLAN
- accessing networks (including security aspects)
- Data Protection Acts
- use of faxes and emails
- video, audio and web conferencing.

● Key terms

Term	Definition
Modem	modulator-demodulator; this is a device that converts digital signals into analogue signals and vice versa.
ADSL	Asymmetric Digital Subscriber Line; asymmetric means that the download speed and upload speed using the internet will be different.
IP address	Internet Protocol address; this is a unique number assigned when a device connects to the internet; it can change each time a device connects.
MAC address	Media Access Control address is a number that identifies a device uniquely; it is usually set at manufacturing stage and is part of the network interface card (NIC).
Wi-Fi	Wireless communication.
Bluetooth	A short-range wireless communication.
WAP	Wireless Access Point; a network transmitter and receiver which allows wireless connection to a network within range of the access points; most networks will have a number of WAPs.
Spread-spectrum frequency hopping	Used in wireless systems, for example, in a Bluetooth system; if a selected communication channel is already being used, another channel is chosen at random.
LAN	Local Area Network
WAN	Wide Area Network
WLAN	Wireless Local Area Network
Social/digital divide	Those people who have the necessary IT skills and/or money to purchase computer equipment have a big advantage over those who do not.
Data packet	Group of data being transmitted (packet contains IP address, ID number, for example).
Authentication	System used to verify that data comes from a secure and trusted source.
Data Protection Act	Legislation set up to protect the rights of the individual about whom data is obtained, stored and processed.
VoIP	Voice over Internet Protocol; allows communication (both verbal and video) using the internet.
Webinar	Web conferencing.

● Networks

When a set of computers have been connected together for the purpose of sharing resources or data, this is known as a computer network.

Cambridge IGCSE ICT Study and Revision Guide © Graham Brown and David Watson, 2017

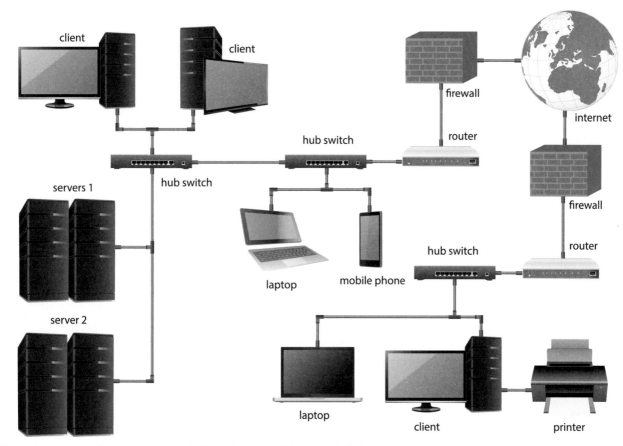

Figure 4.1 Diagram of a computer network, illustrating some of the network devices

Network devices

Modems
A modulator-demodulator is used to convert digital data into analogue data (to allow the data to be transmitted along existing telephone lines); it also converts analogue data into digital data so that incoming data can be understood by the computer. Broadband modems use ADSL; the asymmetric part in this name refers to the fact that the rate at which data can be downloaded is different to the rate at which data can be uploaded. ADSL allows telephone lines to be shared by telephones and computers at the same time.

Hub
This is a device used to connect devices together to form a LAN; it takes the data packet received at one of its ports and sends it to *every* computer on that LAN.

Switch
This is similar to a hub; but this device checks the incoming data packet and works out the destination address and sends the data packet to the computer with that address only.

Router
These are devices that enable data packets to be routed between the different networks, for example, to join a LAN to a WAN. Many routers are wireless in operation.

Routers inspect data packets received over the internet; since all devices on the same network have the same part of an IP address (for example, 109.108.158.1, 109.108.158.2, and so on) the router can send data to the appropriate switch. The switch will then deliver the data packet using the destination address.

Each data packet contains: header, sender and receiver IP addresses, number of data packets in the message and identification number of the packet.

Gateway

This is a network point (node) which acts as an entrance to another network; if a network node needs to communicate outside its own network, it must use a gateway.

Network Interface Card

A Network Interface Card (NIC) is needed to allow a device to connect to a network.

Network cables

Network cables are still used because they allow faster data transfer rates and are usually more secure than wireless connectivity.

IP address

Every time a device connects to a network (for example, the internet) it is given an IP (Internet Protocol) address, for example, 109.108.158.34. If the device logs off, the next time it connects to the network it is supplied with a new IP address.

Devices which never disconnect (for example, web servers) retain the same IP address.

An IP address identifies *where* on the network a device is located.

MAC address

Media Access Control (MAC) addresses are unique to each device; this address is fixed at the manufacturing stage (although it is possible to change the value – this is outside the scope of the syllabus). The MAC address identifies *which* device is connected at a given IP address.

Wi-Fi

This is wireless connectivity. Networks use WAP (wireless access points) to allow users to gain access to the network from anywhere within range. A WAP is a transmitter/receiver which allows a device to communicate with the network. Most networks will have several WAPs, for example, an airport may have hundreds of WAPs to allow passengers to connect to the airport's network from anywhere within the terminal buildings.

Bluetooth

This is also a form of wireless connectivity but it has a very limited range. Bluetooth is often used by tablets, mobile phones and cameras. With this system, the communicating pair of devices will randomly choose 1 of 79 possible channels; if the channel is already in use, a different one is again chosen at random – this is known as *spread-spectrum frequency hopping*.

Local Area Networks

Local Area Networks (LANs) are relatively small networks where all the components are geographically close together (for example, in one building). The devices on a LAN are connected to hubs or switches; one of the hubs or switches will be connected to a router and modem to allow the LAN to be connected to the internet. If two or more LANs are connected together they use a bridge to enable this connection.

Cambridge IGCSE ICT Study and Revision Guide © Graham Brown and David Watson, 2017

Wide Area Networks

Wide Area Networks (WANs) are large networks where the devices are a long way away from each other geographically (for example, in a different city or country); the internet is the most well-known WAN. Since WANs are connected over long distances, they use the public communications network (for example, telephone lines or satellites).

Wireless Local Area Network

A wireless LAN (WLAN) doesn't use any wires or cables to connect devices to the network; wireless nodes (WAPs) are connected into the network at a number of fixed positions and users connect to the network via these nodes.

(NOTE: the advantages and disadvantages of the above network devices are covered in more detail in the Cambridge IGCSE ICT Coursebook.)

● Setting up a network

When setting up a small network the main tasks can be summarised:

- Purchase of all the necessary hardware and software.
- Set up an IP account if internet connection is required.
- Configure all of the hardware and software.
- Install the required software on the server and ensure the network licences have been bought.
- Set up network privileges (for example, network manager).

● Accessing the internet

Users can connect to the internet using desktop computers, laptops, tablets or smartphones/watches. Each device has a number of advantages and disadvantages:

Device	Advantages	Disadvantages
Desktop computers	• faster processors • full-size keyboard and pointing devices • more stable internet connection (usually wired) • all web page features are available	• not very portable; can be used in one fixed position only • requires expensive dongles if the device needs to access the cellular phone network
Laptop computers	• mobile device (single unit) • touchpad is easier to navigate than on tablet/mobile phones • better keyboards than tablets and mobile phones • all web page features are available	• don't have a very good battery life • much heavier and bulkier than tablet or smartphone • processors not as fast as equivalent desktop computer • more expensive than desktop computer for similar specification
Tablets, mobile phones and smartwatches	• very portable and lightweight devices • a person is more likely to have a phone/tablet/watch on their person than a laptop computer • easier to use on the move than a laptop computer • usually have access to either 4G/5G cellular network or Wi-Fi	• small screens and keyboards can cause problems (slower, more error-prone data entry) • small screens often make web pages more difficult to read and navigate • not all websites work properly on tablets and smartphones • signal not as stable as wired laptop/desktop computer

● Common errors

It is very common to see confusion between the terms WAN and WLAN.

✖ A WLAN is a wide area network.
✔ A WLAN is a wireless LAN network; whereas a WAN is a wide area network which may or may not have wireless connectivity.

Confusion between the uses of hubs, switches and routers is very common.

✖ A hub sends an incoming data packet to the correct device on a network. If the hub is connected to the internet it is called a router.

✔ A hub is a device used to connect devices together to form a LAN; it takes the data packet received at one of its ports and sends it to *every* computer on that LAN; a switch is an 'intelligent' hub which sends the data packet only to the correct device on the network. However, routers enable data packets to be routed between the different networks.

IP addresses and MAC addresses are often confused.

✖ An IP address is assigned to a device at the manufacturing stage.

✔ An IP address is assigned to a device by the ISP every time it connects to the network. This allows the location of the device to be determined. MAC addresses are unique to each device; this address is fixed at the manufacturing stage and is usually part of the NIC installed in the device.

Sample exam questions

a   Explain the use of the following network devices:

hub

switch

router.

b   An airport wishes to allow free internet access to all passengers using any of its terminal buildings. Discuss how this can be done.

In your discussion, mention any precautions that need to be taken by airport management and passengers when setting up and accessing the airport network.

Student's answer

a   Hub: used to connect a number of devices together to form a LAN; takes a received data packet and sends it to all the devices on the network.
Switch: as with hubs, connects a number of devices together to form a LAN; each data packet is checked for destination address and data is sent only to the device with this destination address.
Router: allows data packets to be routed between different networks, for example, allows a LAN (or group of LANs) to join a WAN; they check data packets and send them to appropriate switch from where they are sent to the correct device with packet destination address; if the address doesn't match any of the computers connected to that switch, it passes to another switch until the correct device is found.

Examiner's comments

a   The candidate has given a fairly comprehensive answer to the question. They were only required to explain the terms with no need for any comparisons to be made. The addition of diagrams, such as the one below, could prove to be very useful in the explanation (provided it doesn't contradict the text!).

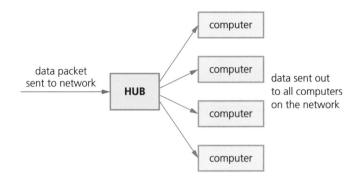

Student's answer

b *Airport can make use of WAPs or 'hot spots'.*
Several WAPs will be located around the airport, allowing passengers to access the network wirelessly.
Passengers need to be aware of security issues when using a shared network.
Passengers should ensure they log off correctly before leaving the network.
Airport management need to be aware of potential virus transmissions and hacking ...
... they will need to set up firewalls that block undesirable websites
... they need to make sure the network has no connections to other networks within the airport that handle security or passenger information (for example, flight lists)
... they need to make sure it is impossible for passengers to gain access to the network that handles flight traffic control.

Examiner's comments

b *This answer needs careful thought. The first part is relatively easy since it only concerns the use of 'hot spots'. The second part hinges on security of the passengers accessing an open network and the care needed by airport management to prevent unauthorised access to security data and traffic control systems.*

> **Examiner's tip**
>
> You will sometimes be asked questions which go beyond your experiences. But if you apply your knowledge of similar situations to the new situation, this shouldn't pose any real problems. In part b, the candidate wouldn't be expected to have covered airport security, but common sense and applying security issues from other applications should allow a good attempt at new, searching questions such as this.

● Network issues and communication

Security

Policing the internet

The Cambridge IGCSE ICT Coursebook covers most of the arguments about whether or not the internet should be policed. The arguments for include:

- To prevent undesirable/dangerous material being accessible to anyone.
- To prevent search engines finding potentially dangerous/undesirable websites.
- Protection of children and the vulnerable.

Cambridge IGCSE ICT Study and Revision Guide © Graham Brown and David Watson, 2017

The main arguments against include:

- It would be expensive to implement.
- It would be difficult to enforce globally.
- Material can already be found elsewhere … the internet just makes it easier to find.
- Freedom of information.
- Laws already exist to protect people against many illegal internet activities.

Authentication

Authentication is used to verify that data comes from a secure and trusted source. Items of authentication include:

- digital certification (see Chapter 8)
- biometrics (see Chapter 8)
- magnetic stripe cards and identity cards.

Identity cards can be contactless (see Chapter 2) and also contain holographic images – a holographic image can appear to move or change colour when viewed from different angles. This makes the illegal replication of the image, for example, by photocopying, much harder.

Passports now usually include an RFID tag, photographs and a holographic image. This helps in airport security to check the validity of the passport and that the passenger is who they claim to be.

Viruses

To help mitigate the risk of viruses, antivirus software should be installed on a computer and constantly *run in the background* to allow the detection of old and new viruses. Most antivirus software has the following features:

- Checking of all files/programs before being loaded or run.
- Use of a database of known viruses to identify potential risks; for this reason, antivirus software needs to be updated on a regular basis.
- Use of *heuristic checking* (checks software for behaviour that could indicate a new virus).
- Problem files/programs are *quarantined* and can be automatically removed or the user can be asked what action they want to take.
- Full scans need to be done at least once a week in case any viruses are time-dependent (for example, only become active on July 4th, and so on).

Other protection against viruses includes using only safe websites, not opening emails that appear suspicious or come from unknown sources; checking for security risks such as phishing and pharming (for more information on this, and on viruses more generally, see Chapter 8).

Communication

Faxes and emails

Electronic faxing and traditional paper-based faxing both still exist. With paper-based systems, the document is first scanned and then the electronic version is sent over the telephone network to another fax machine where it is printed out. Electronic faxing allows a fax to be sent from a computer and is sent to an email account rather than being printed out. This second method is more secure since the document doesn't 'sit' on a fax machine where it can be read by anybody passing by.

Emails are probably one of the most common form of communication. They have the advantage that it is much easier (and quicker) to send the same message to multiple recipients compared to traditional postal systems. Although emails are certainly not instantaneous, they are much faster than conventional post and are also a lot cheaper (no need to buy stamps, paper and envelopes). However, the syntax and spelling of an email address must be *exact*. If not a non-delivery message will be received since the address is incorrect or it could be sent to the wrong person – with potential security issues. However, if normal post is used, this is less of a problem; for example, if an address is: '25 North Street' and it is written on the envelope as '25 Nort Street' the letter would probably still arrive at the correct destination.

Video conferencing

This is a method of communication that uses sound and video. In many cases it removes the need for people to travel to meetings. This is, therefore, safer and less expensive (no travel and accommodation costs), and time isn't lost while important staff are out of the office travelling to meetings. The disadvantages include: possible time lag in communications, expensive hardware to set up and maintain, potential time zone issues and 'loss of perks' due to removal of travel to parts of the world. Required equipment and software includes:

- webcams
- large television screens (the larger the better)
- microphones (not headphones)
- speakers (not headphones)
- CODEC (this encodes/decodes data and also compresses data for transmission)
- echo cancellation software (to prevent unwanted feedback and to synchronise sound and vision).

Audio conferences

This type of communication uses telephones (it is possible to use internet telephones or computers equipped with microphone and speakers). The organiser of the meeting is issued with two PINs by the telephone company. One of the PINs is for their personal use; the second one is sent to all the other delegates along with the time/date of the audio conference. A few minutes before the conference, the organiser calls the meeting number and keys in their PIN, the delegates do the same thing using the PIN sent to them by the organiser, and all are connected on the same telephone call.

Web conferences

These are sometimes referred to as 'webinars'. This method uses computers connected to the internet to allow delegates to communicate by speaking or instant messaging. A 'whiteboard' is used where all delegates can see what is happening during the meeting. The whiteboard allows messages, videos and presentations to be seen by everybody. When one of the delegates wants to talk, send a message or show a video/presentation, they send their request and a 'flag' appears on the organiser's computer; this allows them to control who can talk or write, since it is necessary for the organiser to 'click on' the delegate next to the flag to allow them to actively participate.

● Common errors

It is very common to see candidates making incorrect claims about emails.

- ✖ Once an email has been sent, it instantly appears with the intended recipient.
- ✔ Emails are much quicker to send then physical letters, but there can be delays before an email is delivered, and the email may stay in somebody's inbox for several days before they read it.

It is common to see:

✖ 'Video conferences can be called at any time.'

✔ Video conferences can be called at *short notice* but that is not the same thing as 'called at any time'. Short notice means sending an invitation such as: 'Sorry for the short notice, but can we call a video conference tomorrow at 15:00 please?' Calling a video conference at any time means just going into the video room and starting a conference without checking peoples' availability or diary. These are not the same thing.

Several candidates make incorrect claims about video conferencing:

✖ Video conferencing can be done from the comfort of your own home.

✔ Video conferencing requires a dedicated room with specialist hardware and software. A room also needs to be set up for video conferencing with, for example, proper acoustic panelling in order to work properly. A video call from a smartphone or using VoIP does not require this, and can be done from home. This is not the same as video conferencing.

Sample exam questions

a   Discuss the advantages and disadvantages of using emails compared to sending out mail using conventional post.

b   Discuss the advantages of holding a webinar for training purposes.

Student's answer

a Environmental issues (less paper used, less fuel used driving to the post office, ...).
Emails are much quicker to send.
Emails can be read anywhere in the world if left in the inbox.
More secure than normal post (messages can be encrypted).
Easier to send to multiple recipients.
Recipient can copy/paste message into a document.
Sending emails to a foreign country is much cheaper than postage.
One drawback is the need to buy a computer and pay for an ISP.
If the internet is down, messages can't be sent.
It is possible to send parcels using normal post, something that can't be done using emails.
The recipient may not have a computer.
It doesn't necessarily save money or paper if recipient prints out the message.

Examiner's comments

a The candidate has given at least two advantages and two disadvantages. It is important to give a good, balanced response in questions asking for advantages and disadvantages. Marks can be lost if both sides of the argument are not given.

Student's answer

b No need to travel to a venue for training — saving time and money.
Safer than travelling to venue.
Can bring in 'experts' and 'special guests' whenever needed without having to bring them to the training venue.
Doesn't need special equipment unlike video conferencing.
Easy to use — instant messaging, VoIP, shared videos, and so on.
Organiser has control and can make sure only one person 'talks' at once.
Possible to use tablets and mobile phones, allowing training to take place anywhere.

Cambridge IGCSE ICT Study and Revision Guide © Graham Brown and David Watson, 2017

Examiner's comments

> **Examiner's tips**
>
> - Marks are frequently lost in questions involving comparisons. For example, in part a, if the candidate had written 'It is *easy* to send the same message to a number of recipients' they wouldn't get any marks. The key word here is *easier*, that is, 'It is easier to send the same message …'
>
> - Marks are frequently lost for not making the comparison. It is actually easy sending the same message to a number of people using standard post but it just takes longer and needs more effort, that is, it is not as easy. Be careful with English here!

Exam-style questions

1 a Which devices are being described below? Copy and complete the table. [7 marks]

Description	Network device
A device that takes a data packet received at one of its input ports and sends the data packet to every computer connected to the LAN.	
A device that converts digital data to analogue data (and vice versa) to allow the transmission of data across existing telephone lines.	
A device that connects a LAN to another LAN that uses the same communication protocols.	
A device that takes a data packet received at one of its input ports and works out its destination address; the data packet is then sent to the correct computer on the LAN only.	
A device that enables data to be directed between different networks, for example, to join a LAN to a WAN; the main function is to transmit internet and transmission protocols between two networks.	
A network point (node) that acts as an entrance to another network.	
Hardware which forms part of any device that needs to connect to a network; it often contains the MAC address generated at the manufacturing stage.	

b Describe **four** of the tasks to be done when setting up a small network for the first time. [4 marks]

2 a Explain the **three** terms:

   i LAN

   ii WAN

   iii WLAN [3 marks]

b Copy and complete the tables. In **each** table, tick (✓) **one** of the boxes to indicate your answer.

   i Which of the following is a disadvantage of using a WLAN rather than a normal LAN? [1 mark]

Printer queues can cause a big problem	
If the main server breaks down, the whole network goes down	
Data transfer rate is much slower	
All computers can have access to the same software and files	

ii Which of the following is the meaning of the term **MAC**?   [1 mark]

Medium access card	
Media address command	
Modem addressing card	
Media access control	

iii Which of the following isn't part of a data packet?   [1 mark]

Sender's IP address	
Time and date the data packet was sent	
Identity number of the data packet	
Header to identify the data packet	

3 a Copy and complete the following sentences using **one** of the words or phrases given below (note: four of them will not be used):

anti-piracy law Data Protection Act heuristic checking   asymmetric

digital divide hologram   authentication   false positive

3-D printing dial-up modem   handshaking

i   Checking of software for types of behaviour that could indicate a possible virus is known as …

ii When a user knows that a file/program which has been identified as infected with a virus is, in fact, not infected, this is known as a …

iii A 3-D image formed from laser light; the image produced where the two laser light beams meet on a photographic plate is known as …

iv People who have the necessary IT skills and money to purchase and use computers, which gives these people an advantage over those who do not is called …

v   Verification that data comes from a secure and trusted source on the internet is called …

vi System to protect the rights of the individual about whom information is obtained, stored and processed is known as …

vii The type of subscriber telephone line where download rate of data is different to upload rate of data is called …   [7 marks]

b Give **two** reasons why the internet should be policed and **two** reasons why it shouldn't.   [4 marks]

The effects of using ICT

CHAPTER 5

Key objectives

The objectives of this chapter are to revise:

- the effects of ICT on employment
- the effects of ICT on working patterns
- microprocessor-controlled devices used in the home.

● Key terms

Term	Definition
Full-time working	A full-time employee has ongoing employment and works, on average, around 38 hours each week. The actual hours of work for an employee in a particular job or industry are agreed between the employer and the employee.
Part-time working	Staff work fewer hours per week than full-time staff; this is due to either fewer hours per day or fewer days per week.
Flexi-time	Staff can start work and finish work at different times to normal staff; however, they must work the full hours for the day.
Job sharing	The full-time job is divided between two workers, who work half the weekly hours each; their combined hours are equal to the hours of a full-time member of staff.
Compressed hours	The employee works the full hours for the week but works longer days than normal; thus they could compress five days of normal working into four days of longer hours.

● Employment

ICT has had a large effect on employment in the following areas:

- manufacturing
- retail
- banking
- office work.

This has led to a number of job losses.

Manufacturing

The use of robotics has taken over many manual tasks previously done by employees, for example, in the manufacture of cars, electronic equipment, and so on. Robotics leads to greater productivity, more consistency, non-stop working and no strike action. However, robots are expensive to buy and maintain and are unable to respond to unusual circumstances which are outside their programming.

There are positive job opportunities for computer technicians, programmers, systems analysts and network managers, however, as well as more jobs for quality control, and so on.

Retail and banking

Websites now allow people to buy online rather than visiting the shops in town. This has of course resulted in the closure of some shops, particularly those that have been unable to adapt and offer both online shopping and high street shopping. The same is true of banking, where many people bank online and even manage accounts and make payments using smartphone/tablet banking Apps.

Office work

Administration, human resources and payroll have been severely affected by ICT. This is due to the use of software such as spreadsheets, word processors and databases.

Word processors have removed the need for filing clerks and work can also be moved to countries where labour costs are lower.

Spreadsheets have allowed salary/wage calculations, analysis and production of graphs to be done automatically. Data from 'clocking in' devices and from databases allows for a fully automatic salary system. Education can also make use of this software to monitor the progress of students.

Databases have allowed personnel departments to do cross-checking of staff skills, making recruitment and promotion much easier and quicker.

The software has reduced the need to have as many staff but has opened up opportunities in training, web designing, improved customer relations, and so on.

● Working patterns

Introduction of ICT into the workplace has led to a number of changes in working patterns for staff:

The definition of each of these work patterns is given in the Key Terms box.

- full-time working
- part-time working
- flexi-time working
- job sharing
- compressed hours.

(Note: shift work is different; this is where a company works 24/7 and they have, for example, three shifts of eight hours over each 24-hour period – each member of staff does a full-time job but their hours vary depending on which shift they are doing.)

If full-time working is defined as eight hours per day (40 hours per week) from 8 a.m. to 4 p.m., then:

- part-time working could be five hours per day (for example, 10 a.m. to 3 p.m.)
- flexi-time could be eight hours from 11 a.m. to 7 p.m. each day
- job sharing could be:
  worker 1: 8 a.m. to 4 p.m. Monday and Tuesday and 8 a.m. to 12 noon on Wednesday
  worker 2: 12 noon to 4 p.m. on Wednesday and 8 a.m. to 4 p.m. Thursday and Friday.

● Microprocessor-controlled devices in the home

Labour-saving devices are now operated using embedded chips (microprocessors), for example, automatic ovens, washing machines and dishwashers. These are all regarded as labour-saving devices and have the advantages that:

- people don't need to stay at home while food is cooking or clothes/dishes are being washed
- people have more leisure time
- it leads to a healthier lifestyle (smart fridges and freezers, for example)
- it is possible to operate appliances remotely using smartphone/tablet Apps when away from home.

The main drawbacks are that they:

- tend to make people lazy
- can lead to an unhealthy lifestyle (ready-made microwave meals)
- can mean people become less fit due to less exercise
- result in loss of certain skills.

Other devices, not termed labour-saving, also have inbuilt microchips which make them work more efficiently and also give them features which would be impossible without the technology. These include: televisions, cameras, air conditioning units and CD/DVD players, for example.

Figure 5.1 Examples of labour-saving devices

● Common errors

- It is very common to see confusion between the terms 'part-time', 'flexi-time' and 'compressed hours'; the best way to avoid confusion is to look at the examples given above.
- Many candidates regard televisions and cameras as labour-saving devices. To decide if an appliance falls into this category, just ask the question: 'Is there any advantage in having embedded chips so that the appliance can be operated when nobody is at home?'

Sample exam questions

a Normal full-time staff work from 10 a.m. to 6 p.m. Monday to Friday. Explain the meaning of the following terms, giving examples:

part-time working

compressed hours

flexi-time working.

b Explain how ICT has affected jobs in the car manufacturing industry.

Student's answer

a Part-time: staff work fewer hours per day than full-time staff, for example, 1 p.m. to 5 p.m. each day.
Compressed hours: staff work the full hours for the week but work from, for example, 9 a.m. to 7 p.m. each day Monday to Thursday; they don't work on Fridays.
Flexi-time: staff work the full eight hours per day but start and finish at different times compared to full-time staff, for example, 8 a.m. to 4 p.m. each day.

Examiner's comments

a The candidate has correctly chosen timings that reflect the different work patterns. The examples given tie up with the descriptions, which is of course very important.

Student's answer

b *Greater unemployment.*
  Need to retrain staff in other work or to 'work with' robots.
  Many jobs in areas such as quality control now exist.
  There is a better working environment (cleaner and not as noisy).
  Possible moving of jobs to other countries.

Examiner's comments

b The candidate has given *both* advantages and disadvantages; it is very important to try
   and give as balanced an answer as possible.

Examiner's tip
When giving examples as part of your answer, always make sure that the examples
don't conflict with any descriptions, otherwise marks could be lost even if your
descriptions are correct.

Exam-style questions

1 a Describe **two** advantages and **two** disadvantages of using robots
      in manufacturing.   [4 marks]

   b Give **three** advantages of using microprocessors in labour-saving
      devices used in the home.   [3 marks]

2 a Explain the following terms:

      part-time working

      flexi-time working

      job sharing

      compressed hours.   [4 marks]

   b Describe the advantages to a company and its staff of adopting flexible
      working patterns.   [3 marks]

   c Describe **three** disadvantages to the general public of having electronic
      devices fitted with embedded microprocessors which can be controlled
      using an App from, for example, a smartphone.   [3 marks]

CHAPTER 6 — ICT applications

Key objectives

The objectives of this chapter are to revise:

- communication applications
- data handling applications
- school management systems
- measurement applications
- microprocessors in control applications
- modelling applications
- manufacturing
- booking systems
- banking applications
- expert systems
- computers in medicine
- computers in libraries
- automatic stock control
- recognition systems
- monitoring and tracking systems
- use of satellites in GPS, GIS and media communications.

● Key terms

Term	Definition
Tweening	The generation of intermediate frames between images – this gives the impression that the first image evolves slowly into the second image.
Morphing	The procedure where one image is changed into another image in a smooth way (morphing uses tweening to give the transition effect).
Rendering	The generation of an image from a model using software.
SIM card	Subscriber Identity Module chip – allows a device to connect to the mobile cellular network.
Radio buttons	This is an 'icon' (for example, a circle) which is used to represent an option on an online form; (for example: ○ female ● male) – only one of the options may be chosen.
ADC	Analogue to Digital Converter
DAC	Digital to Analogue Converter
Sensor	Device that inputs data to a computer/microprocessor, usually in analogue format; the data is a measurement of some physical quantity.
(Computer) modelling	Creation of a model of a real system in order to study the behaviour of the system; the model is based on mathematical representations and algorithms.
e-ticket	An electronic ticket, for example, in the form of an email or QR code sent to a mobile phone/tablet – it acts in the same way as a paper ticket.
ATM	Automatic Teller Machine
EFT	Electronic Funds Transfer
IBDE	Inter-Bank Data Exchange – an encrypted filing system used by banks.
EFTPOS	Electronic Funds Transfer (at the) Point-Of-Sale
Knowledge base	A type of database used in an expert system which allows for the collection, organisation and retrieval of knowledge from human experts.
Rules base	Knowledge is represented as a set of rules; each rule shows a connection between the data stored in the knowledge base; makes use of IF … THEN structure to determine the next step to take.
Inference engine	This interprets input data by checking the data against the rules and logic stored in the knowledge base.
Explanation system	This explains to the user the reasoning process carried out by the expert system when arriving at its conclusions.
CT scan	Computed Tomography scanning system.
MRI scan	Magnetic Resonance Imaging scanning system.
Prosthetics	Imitation limbs to replace damaged or lost limbs in humans.
ANPR	Automatic Number Plate Recognition system.
GPS	Global Positioning Satellite
GIS	Geographic Information System

● Communication, data handling and school management applications

Communication applications

Paper-based systems

Flyers, posters and newsletters can easily be produced using word processors, desktop publishing and a standard printer. They can then be distributed in a number of ways to target the required audience.

Brochures can be a single folded sheet or a stapled booklet – these may require professional printing since they often need to use glossy paper. Posters can be a very large size so that they can be placed on advertising hoardings on the side of the road, for example.

Websites

Rather than printing advertising material, websites can be used instead. This requires the company to develop its own website or pay to have its adverts on another company's website. Although producing paper-based advertising material is expensive, hiring a website developer is also an expensive consideration. However, advertising material that is presented in an electronic format is much easier and quicker to update, and won't need to be reprinted. Websites can also have a global audience, for example, advertising on social networking sites, and can make use of multimedia elements.

Multimedia presentations

Presentations on a multimedia projector have many advantages; they can include a number of multimedia elements such as animation, video and sound, and they can also be interactive. Such elements mean that presentations and adverts can be tailored for selected audiences. Large screens are used so they can also be very eye catching, but such equipment can be expensive. Multimedia presentations like this can be found in shopping malls, offices and classrooms.

Music scores

Music can communicate a lot to an audience. A catchy or well-known song can increase the impact of an advert significantly, while the score of a film can, for example, tell the audience if the on-screen character is happy, sad or in danger. Music scores make considerable use of ICT:

- Use of sampling, mixers and synthesisers
- Generating music scores by use of software
- There is no real need to understand music notation to produce music.

Cartoons and animation

Animation (which makes use of techniques such as tweening, morphing and rendering) is now produced on computers using very sophisticated software. Cartoons and animation can add humour and it is also possible to do things with cartoon characters that are not possible with humans. Indeed, the 'humanisation' of animals is a very common and successful technique used in advertising (just look at the many television and cinema adverts that use this). Animation tends to be moving whereas cartoons tend to be static, but the two terms often overlap. It is, however, very important that the animation or cartoon doesn't distract the customer so much that the actual message in the advert is lost.

Mobile phones

Mobile phones have become one of the major ways for people to communicate. It is now difficult to imagine a world without them. Due to their small size they can be carried around anywhere and they allow communication from almost any part of the world. They allow phone conversations, video calls, text messaging, sending/receiving emails and many other features. They either use the 4G/5G cellular network or wireless 'hot spots'.

Internet telephony

Phoning somebody using a computer has also become increasingly popular. This uses Voice over Internet Protocol (VoIP) technology and can allow conversations using an internet phone connected to a computer or using the built-in microphone and speakers. Data is sent over the internet in the form of data packets. It is possible to connect to somebody on a landline phone, mobile phone or another computer using this technology. One of the big advantages is the very low cost of the calls; but sometimes the quality is poor (echoing, drop out and loud interference noises are the main issues).

Business cards/letter heads

Many websites offer to produce business cards and headed notepaper. These give companies a more professional look and can also contain important information, such as contact numbers, and be used as a form of advertising.

Data handling applications

Surveys

Questionnaires and surveys are often used in market research. Questionnaires can be either paper-based or online. If printed forms are used, the information is read using either OCR or OMR input devices (explored in detail in Chapter 2). If online, the form will use radio buttons, dropdown menus or restricted text boxes to gather the data.

Address lists

Computers, tablets and smartphones are used to store personal data such as telephone numbers, birthdays, email addresses, and so on. By storing such data electronically, it is much easier to group people together based on one parameter (for example, grouping family members together for data of a personal nature).

Clubs and society records

Information about members of clubs or societies is often stored on electronic databases. This makes it easier to contact people when a particular event comes up – the database would filter out certain information so that only the appropriate people would be sent invitations, for example. Mail merging would be used to find email addresses or postal addresses. It is important to remember that the information stored would need to conform to the appropriate Data Protection Act.

Record keeping is a similar application where customer details would be held on a database. For example, if a particular author has just published a new book, a book shop could easily contact customers who'd previously purchased titles by that author in order to inform them of the latest book release.

School reports

Computers can be used in schools to store personal details, academic performance or attendance records. This makes it much quicker to produce end-of-term reports, and can also make them look more professional.

Cambridge IGCSE ICT Study and Revision Guide © Graham Brown and David Watson, 2017

School management systems

As mentioned earlier, computers can be used in schools in a variety of ways.
These include:

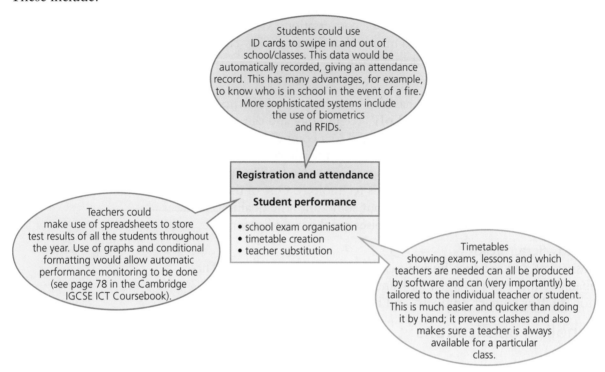

Students could use
ID cards to swipe in and out of
school/classes. This data would be
automatically recorded, giving an attendance
record. This has many advantages, for example,
to know who is in school in the event of a fire.
More sophisticated systems include
the use of biometrics
and RFIDs.

Registration and attendance

Student performance

• school exam organisation
• timetable creation
• teacher substitution

Teachers could
make use of spreadsheets to store
test results of all the students throughout
the year. Use of graphs and conditional
formatting would allow automatic
performance monitoring to be done
(see page 78 in the Cambridge
IGCSE ICT Coursebook).

Timetables
showing exams, lessons and which
teachers are needed can all be produced
by software and can (very importantly) be
tailored to the individual teacher or student.
This is much easier and quicker than doing
it by hand; it prevents clashes and also
makes sure a teacher is always
available for a particular
class.

● Common errors

Candidates generally have difficulty deciding the best way to advertise
products and services: leaflets, websites, telephone advertising, shopping mall
presentations or on television/cinema. A greater awareness of advertising in
your own area could help eliminate such errors in exams.

> **Examiner's tip**
>
> It's hard to decide the best way to advertise products and services. Think about the
> adverts and advertising you see in your local area to get some ideas!

Sample exam questions

a A company manufactures toys. It needs to decide whether to advertise its
new toys using flyers and brochures or to advertise using its own website.
Explain the relative advantages and disadvantages of the two methods.

b The same company also wants feedback on its new toy designs from the
general public. It can either use paper questionnaires (using OMR to collect
the data) or have an online form using its own website. Discuss the relative
advantages and disadvantages of the two methods.

Student's answer

a Flyers:
- can be produced using a word processor and desktop publishing and using the company's own printer
- can ensure only the target audience receives the advertisements
- can be inserted into weekly/monthly magazines
- paper documents need no special equipment to read them
- paper documents can easily be thrown away as junk mail
- there is the cost of delivery to consider
- advertising is limited to local area.

Website:
- available to a global audience
- possible to include multimedia elements
- can include links to other websites
- can make use of 'hit counters' to see how many times its website was visited
- much easier and quicker to update the website when new products are developed
- expensive to set up and maintain
- not everybody has access to a computer or knows how to use one
- there are the usual risks of hacking and pharming which could affect its website.

Examiner's comments

a The answer required some explanation of the advantages and disadvantages of both methods. The candidate has correctly given at least two examples of each, leading to a fairly well-balanced response.

Student's answer

b Paper:
- paper forms can be handed out anywhere
- a very quick method of gathering information
- OMR stops customers adding additional useful information
- there is the risk of errors in the filling out the questionnaires
- can't tailor the questionnaire to the individual.

Online:
- a very quick way of gathering and analysing data
- allows for automatic analysis
- can be tailored to suit the individual based on previous responses
- easier for customer to amend an error
- potentially more expensive to set up
- need some way to get people to visit the company's website in the first place
- hacking could lead to forms being 'modified'.

Conclusion: I would use the online method to gather information since it is faster to analyse the data and the information is probably more accurate.

Examiner's comments

b Again a number of advantages and disadvantages are given, leading to a reasonably balanced answer. An attempt at a conclusion was made (the question asked candidates to discuss) based on the answers already given – this would make their conclusion valid.

Cambridge IGCSE ICT Study and Revision Guide © Graham Brown and David Watson, 2017

● Measurement, control and modelling applications

Measurement applications

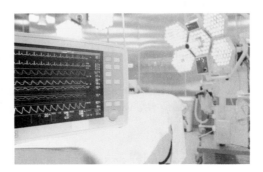

Figure 6.1 Example measurement devices

Measurement applications use sensors and microprocessors/computers to monitor a process. Sensors take measurements from the real world (for example, temperature, light, rate of rotation, and so on) and send the data to the microprocessor/computer. Most often an ADC is needed as the sensor data is usually in analogue form.

The data is then checked against pre-stored data in memory and the files are updated together with some form of output, such as on screen, printouts or warning sounds/lights. The microprocessor/computer will take no action to change any of the conditions during the measurement process.

Here are three examples:

Example 1: weather stations
- Sensors are used to measure rainfall, temperature, wind speed, wind direction, air pressure and air humidity.
- Data is gathered 24/7, converted to digital and then sent to a computer.
- The computer processes the data using stored data/previous weather patterns and predicts the weather for the next few days.

Example 2: monitoring patients' vital signs in a hospital ward
- Sensors are used to read key data such as pulse rate, heart rate, temperature.
- Data is converted to digital (by an ADC) and sent to a computer.
- Sensor data is compared to pre-determined values stored in the computer's memory.
- The results are output on a screen as numbers or as a moving graph.
- Alarms are activated if any parameter being measured is outside an acceptable range.
- Monitoring of the patient continues until the sensors are removed from the patient.

Example 3: river pollution
- This is similar to the examples above; this time pH, temperature and oxygen content of the river are measured using sensors placed at different places in the river.

- The data is collected over a set period and is stored in a data logger at the side of the river; this data is either gathered by scientists (by downloading results) or it is automatically transmitted to the main computer in the environmental laboratory.
- Data stored in the memory from previous days is compared to the newly gathered data and graphs are produced showing the trends in each of the measured parameters.

Computers are used to do monitoring since they 'won't forget to take readings', they can take more frequent readings 24/7, they can automatically analyse data and produce graphs, and they are also inherently safer (for example, removes the chance of somebody falling in the river).

Control applications

Figure 6.2 Example control devices

As with measurement applications, control applications use sensors, microprocessors/computers and other devices, such as actuators. Again, the sensor data is sent to a microprocessor/computer (usually after conversion to digital using an ADC) where it is compared to pre-stored data. If the sensor data is outside the acceptable range (for example, temperature > pre-stored value OR < pre-stored value) then the microprocessor/computer will take action. This is usually a signal sent out to an actuator, for example, to switch a heater on or off, turn a pump on or off, and so on. The data is gathered constantly and is analysed by the microprocessor/computer continuously to maintain the correct conditions in whatever process is being controlled. Essentially, the output from the microprocessor/computer affects the next input it receives.

Here are four examples:

Example 1: automatic oven
- Sensors are used to measure temperature; also a timer is used where necessary.
- If a timer is used, start time and end time are entered by the user and the microprocessor compares these values with the current time so that the oven is started and stopped as required.
- Sensor values (temperature, in this case) are sent to the microprocessor, which decides whether or not the heating elements need to be switched on or off to maintain the correct temperature for the cooking process.

Example 2: central heating
- Central heating systems either use electric heaters or they control hot water pumped to radiators around the building; sensors send temperature readings of the room to the microprocessor in both methods.
- If electric heaters are used then the control is similar to Example 1 above.
- With the second type, the microprocessor sends signals to start the pump if the temperature falls below that set by the user …

- … Or it sends signals to stop the pumps once the temperature readings are above or equal to the required temperature.
- The user will key in the required temperature for the room(s); the microprocessor will also control the temperature of the water being pumped around the radiators.

Example 3: a chemical process
- Chemical processes can involve temperature control (switching heating elements on or off), pressure (opening or closing valves to maintain pressure), pH (opening or closing valves to admit acid/alkali to the process), and so on.
- Sensors send data (via an ADC) to a computer, which has pre-set values for all necessary parameters stored in memory.
- By comparing sensor data with pre-stored values, the computer can control the process as described in the first bullet point.

Example 4: glasshouse (greenhouse) environmental control
- Sensors are used to measure temperature, air humidity, soil moisture, light levels and soil pH.
- Data is gathered 24/7 and is sent to a microprocessor via an ADC.
- The microprocessor compares the sensor data with pre-stored values and takes the necessary action to maintain the correct environmental conditions in the glasshouse/greenhouse (please refer to Chapter 6.4.4 in the Cambridge IGCSE ICT Coursebook to see how the correct conditions are maintained).

Turtle graphics
This is based on LOGO, where a 'turtle' is used to draw geometric shapes on screen or on paper. A number of commands such as FORWARD *x*, RIGHT *t*, PENUP and REPEAT *n* are used to control the turtle. You will usually be given these commands on the exam paper unless the question requires you to actually name and describe LOGO commands.

The following example draws a square with sides of 30 units:

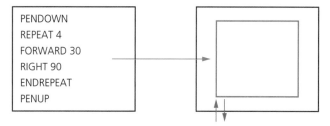

```
PENDOWN
REPEAT 4
FORWARD 30
RIGHT 90
ENDREPEAT
PENUP
```

Modelling applications

A computer model is the creation of a model of a real system in order to study the behaviour of the system under varying conditions. The model is computer-generated and is based on mathematical representations and algorithms. They can be quite simple (for example, using a spreadsheet) or complex (requiring very complex software).

The whole idea is to try to find out what mechanisms control how a system behaves. They tend to save money and can help find solutions more quickly, often in a safer manner.

Sometimes modelling is done on a spreadsheet if it involves simple mathematical modelling (for example,

Figure 6.3 Crash simulation computer model

a school tuck shop takings, population growth, check out queues in a supermarket, and so on). Complex modelling is often called a 'simulation', where a computer model is used to simulate how a real-life process works under varying conditions. For example:

- Simulating traffic light timings at a busy junction.
- Simulating the flight of a spacecraft to Mars.
- Simulating a nuclear or chemical process.
- Simulating car crashes.

They all have the benefit of being safer than doing the real thing (even if it were possible in some cases) and allow various scenarios to be tried first without causing any risks to people or equipment. This often has cost benefits since building the real thing can be expensive and the possibility of finding solutions to problems faster can also have potential cost savings.

● Common errors

Many candidates don't fully understand the role of sensors in control applications.

✖ Sensors in control applications only send data to the microprocessor/ computer when something happens.
✔ Sensors constantly send data to microprocessors/computers and it is these devices that make the control decisions about, for example, opening/ closing valves in a control application.

Sample exam questions

a Describe how sensors and a microprocessor can be used to control a rocket engine where a valve is opened to admit more fuel if the thrust is less than 5 million newtons. Sensors are used to measure the thrust.

b Describe four reasons why a process may be modelled.

Student's answer

a Sensor sends data to microprocessor via ADC.
  Microprocessor compares sensor data with stored data.
  If sensor data <5 million newtons, microprocessor sends signals …
  … to actuators to open the fuel valve.
  If sensor data ≥5 million newtons, microprocessor sends signals …
  … to actuators to close fuel valve.
  System continues until rocket engine has finished burn.

Examiner's comments

a Questions of this type always have key steps:
  - Sensor data is continuously taken.
  - Sensor data is converted to digital.
  - Microprocessor/computer compares data with pre-stored values.
  - If sensor data out of range, microprocessor/computer sends signals …
  - … to open/close valves, switches, and so on.

Cambridge IGCSE ICT Study and Revision Guide © Graham Brown and David Watson, 2017

Student's answer

b Models are often less expensive than building the real system.

It is often safer to use a model than a real system.

It is easier/faster to try different scenarios rather than trying them on a real system.

Some real systems being modelled have a very large time frame (for example, climate change) therefore modelling is a much quicker method to use.

Some tasks are almost impossible to do in real life (for example, flying a rocket to Mars).

Examiner's comments

b The candidate gave five answers when only four were requested in the question. This is okay provided the first four are correct, since subsequent answers would be ignored (even if correct).

Examiner's tip

It is often a good idea to use 'bullet points' when answering questions of the type in part a. This also helps examiners and is easier to make sure you include all the steps necessary in the control application.

● Manufacturing, booking systems and banking systems

Manufacturing

Manufacturing is an area where ICT has had a very large impact over the years … from marketing all the way through to manufacturing itself. Some of the impacts of ICT have been covered earlier on; this section will look at the effect of introducing robotics.

Robots can do many of the tasks hitherto done by skilled humans, for example, welding metals, spray painting items, assembly of electronic components, and so on. Once a robot has been 'trained' to do a specific task, it will go on doing the same task 24/7 with identical accuracy and consistency each time. They only need breaks if a fault develops or their maintenance schedule demands it. Although expensive to buy and to maintain, robots are still cheaper than paying humans and, due to their greater speed in carrying out tasks, they increase productivity.

Booking systems

Online booking systems include:

- theatre
- cinema
- hotels/holidays
- transport (flights, trains and coaches).

Anywhere where it is important that 'double booking' can't take place is best done using ICT. With the old manual systems, it was almost impossible to prevent double booking until checks were done at the end of the day, which often meant rescheduling.

When booking seats or hotel rooms, customers will be asked to initially give key data such as dates, times, names of people, method of payment, and so on. The system will then check the availability of seats or hotel rooms which match the customer's requirements. If everything checks out all right, the customer can accept the booking and then make payment. Once the customer accepts the booking, the seats (or hotel room) are 'flagged' on a database as now being unavailable, thus preventing any possibility of double booking.

An email will then be sent back to the customer as a form of confirmation; this also acts as their e-ticket. Sometimes a QR code is sent through to a mobile phone or tablet instead. The QR code will contain all of the necessary data regarding the booking. For example:

```
Flight         : JK1532 Airbus A320
Outbound       : August 25 2017
Gates close    : 17:40 T3
Destination    : Bucharest Otopeni (BUH)
Passenger name : E. Ducation
Ref No         : JKG345SD21F
```

Confirmation QR code

Figure 6.4 QR code mobile confirmation

The advantages and disadvantages of online booking systems are covered in great depth in Chapter 6.8 of the Cambridge IGCSE ICT Coursebook.

Banking systems

Computer technology has greatly affected how we now do our daily banking:

- Use of ATMs to get cash and carry out many other banking operations
- Internet banking
- Telephone banking
- Chip and PIN
- Clearing of bank cheques (checks)
- EFT
- Use of phone Apps to make payments.

ATMs

ATMs allow customers to carry out a number of tasks without having to visit their actual bank. They can withdraw cash, change their PIN, get a balance, request a statement, top up a mobile phone, transfer money/make a payment, and so on. Once a customer inserts their card into the ATM slot, the following stages are carried out:

- The bank details are read from the chip.
- Card validity (is it stolen, has expiry date been exceeded, has the card been blocked, and so on) is checked.
- Some accounts give the customer a choice of language.
- The customer will be asked to key in their four-digit PIN.
- The keyed-in PIN is compared to the one stored on the chip on the card.
- If the PINs match, the customer is allowed to proceed and the next screen appears.
- If the PIN is incorrect, the customer gets two more attempts before the transaction is terminated (some ATMs retain the card at this point as well).
- When the next screen appears, the customer will be asked to select what service they require.

- If they want cash, it will give a list of available amounts or ask the customer to give a different amount in multiples of 10.
- The machine will count out the cash and at the same time return the card.
- Once the customer takes their card, the cash will be ejected.
- Other options can of course be chosen; whatever option is selected requires the ATM to contact the customer's bank to check for sufficient funds, and so on.
- Once the customer is finished they take their card.

Internet banking

Internet banking requires high levels of security to protect both the customer and the bank. Customers can carry out most tasks online (apart from get cash!) which means that banking can be done 24/7 without the need to travel to their bank. Provided they can find internet access, customers can do their banking from anywhere in the world.

Coupled to internet banking is online shopping where customers pay for goods or services online. This widens customer choice and allows 24/7 shopping.

Disadvantages of online banking and shopping include: closing down of shops and banks in high streets, increased internet fraud, health risks (lack of exercise), greater possibility of mismanaging accounts and the usual security risks of hacking and pharming.

Banks and shops save money (as they need fewer branches or shops which require expensive rent) and they can now have access to global markets. The setting up of websites (including security issues) is a costly exercise and it has potentially reduced loyalty from customers since they no longer get a personal service.

Telephone banking/use of Apps

With telephone banking, a customer can carry out many banking actions by telephoning the bank's helpline. Some of the facilities, such as finding out your balance, are done automatically without the need to talk to anybody. Different banks have different systems in place, but generally:

- Call the bank and use the options to choose telephone banking.
- Key in your account number or 16-digit debit card number.
- Many banks then ask for certain digits from a telephone banking PIN (for example, you may be asked for the second and fifth digit to continue).
- You are then given a number of options.

This is slower than internet banking since there may be a queue on the helpline due to several people needing access.

Mobile phones also allow people to make payments using Apps on their phone. For example, it is possible:

- to cancel standing orders and Direct Debits
- to increase or decrease standing order payment amounts
- to use the *Touch ID fingerprint sensor* on certain smartphones
- to make bill payments to existing beneficiaries and transfer funds between accounts displayed within the App
- to view transactions that are pending on accounts
- to view balances and the last 90 transactions, for example.

Chip and PIN

Chip and PIN is more secure than the older magnetic stripe technology (refer to Chapter 2 for more information on magnetic stripes). The operation of the chip and PIN system when making a purchase is discussed in great detail in the Cambridge IGCSE ICT Coursebook, but an outline is given below (which shows what happens when a customer pays for a meal in a restaurant):

Figure 6.5 A handheld chip and PIN machine

- The card is inserted into the chip and PIN machine and the customer checks the amount and then presses OK; they are then asked to enter their PIN.
- The entered PIN is checked against the PIN stored on the chip embedded in the card; the card is also checked at this stage for its validity.
- If the PINs match correctly, the bank's computer is contacted to see if the customer has sufficient funds; if the PINs don't match correctly, the transaction is terminated.
- If everything proves to be satisfactory, the transaction is authorised and is given a unique transaction code.
- Money is then deducted from the customer's account and the same amount is added to the restaurant's bank account.

Clearing of cheques

Bank cheques use MICR technology (see Chapter 2). The clearing of cheques requires the use of special characters at the bottom of the cheques; for example:

These characters are printed in a type of ink that contains magnetisable particles of an iron alloy. When the cheque is passed over an MICR the following happens:

- The MICR characters are recognised.
- The ink in the special characters is first magnetised.
- The characters are then passed over an MICR read head and each character produces a unique magnetic waveform.
- Each waveform is recognised by the computer which means the character has been read.

Cheques are then gathered together at the end of the day and sent to a central cheque clearing house where the following stages occur:

- The cheque is scanned for the amount of money, account number, sort code and cheque number.
- The cheque is given a digital signature (using IBDE, the Inter-Bank Data Exchange; an encrypted filing system used by banks); using the sort code, the cheque is then sent to another clearing house (the clearing house of the bank which is paying out).
- The digital signature is then checked and the cheque is passed through the bank's own MICR reader, where the sort code is used to sort cheques into branch order.
- The bank checks that the customer has sufficient funds to cover the cheque and it also checks the authenticity of the customer's signature and the date on the cheque.
- If everything is correct, the bank pays the bank that presented the cheque for payment.
- If there are problems (for example, not enough funds, forgery, not signed or dated, and so on), the cheque is returned unpaid.

Electronic Funds Transfer (EFT)

EFT allows *money transfer instructions* to be done using a computer. No actual money is transferred. When an EFT instruction is received, the computer system automatically decreases one account by an agreed sum of money and also increases the recipient's account with the same amount.

● Common errors

The characters at the bottom of cheques are not magnetised until they pass through an MICR reader; very few candidates realise that the ink used is *magnetisable* and isn't actually *magnetised* to represent the characters until the reading process takes place.

Many candidates don't fully understand the EFT process:

✘ During an EFT money is actually moved from one account to another.

✔ During EFT an instruction is sent to the computer which results in the customer's account being decreased by a sum of money. The account of the person being paid is increased by this same amount as part of this process. No money is actually moved during the process. The accounts of both customer and company are updated to reflect the transaction taking place.

Sample exam questions

a   Describe the advantages of booking a flight online.

b   Describe the process when a person pays for an item at a shop till using a debit card containing an embedded chip.

Student's answer

a Prevents the possibility of double booking.
  Customer gets immediate feedback on availability of seats on chosen flight.
  Customer can make bookings at any time of day.
  Easier to browse aeroplane seating plans to choose desired seat(s).
  Possible to reserve a seat for a period of time before finally deciding.
  Makes use of e-tickets.
  Allows use of modern smartphone Apps technology where customer is sent a QR containing all flight information/confirmation.

Examiner's comments

a Since only the advantages are asked for, there is no need to make any comparisons
   between online and older manual systems.

Student's answer

b Validity of card first checked.
  PIN entered and compared to PIN stored on embedded chip.
  If PIN is correct, transaction proceeds.
  Shop's bank contacts customer's bank.
  Check made to see if customer has sufficient funds.
  If card not valid, or insufficient funds or incorrect PIN, then transaction is
  terminated.
  If all checks prove satisfactory, the transaction is authorised and a unique
  authorisation code is generated.
  Money for item being bought is then deducted from customer's bank account…
  … And the same amount of money is added to the shop's bank account.

Examiner's comments

b The candidate has correctly attempted to put the stages when paying by chip and PIN
   in the correct order; the question doesn't necessarily ask for correct order and marks
   wouldn't be deducted if the order wasn't correct.

Cambridge IGCSE ICT Study and Revision Guide © Graham Brown and David Watson, 2017

● Expert systems and medical applications

Expert systems

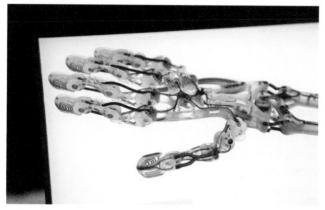

Figure 6.6 3-D printed medical applications

These have been developed to mimic the expertise and knowledge of experts in a particular field. For example:

- medical diagnosis
- engine diagnostics
- oil and mineral prospecting
- tax and financial calculations
- strategy games (for example, chess)
- identification of plants, animals
- identification of chemical structures
- road scheduling for delivery
- vehicles (logistics).

Expert systems consist of a knowledge base, rules base, inference engine, explanation system and an interactive user interface (refer to definitions in Key Terms at the beginning of this chapter).

Expert systems are used since they can speed up the time it takes to solve a problem and they never forget to ask a pertinent question as part of the analysis. There is less need for specialists in many cases, which saves money and also means expert systems can be used in developing countries. However, they do tend to lack the common sense approach and also lack emotional reasoning – often a crucial element in medical diagnosis. To use an expert system effectively requires considerable training and it is essential to ensure they are properly set up to avoid errors in the decisions made.

Computers in medicine

Record keeping databases are used in hospitals to store accurate records about patients. These records are shared by other medical practitioners and pharmacists. Such centralisation is crucial in the case of emergencies and stopping the prescription of drugs which can interact in an unsafe manner.

Monitoring patients

The monitoring of patients was covered earlier in this chapter. The benefits of using sensors and computers to monitor patients in hospital include:

- It reduces the risk of errors.
- The system can operate 24/7 without getting tired.
- They never 'forget' to take a reading.
- Readings can be taken more frequently.
- Computer systems can react much more quickly to a change in patient circumstances.
- The system can automatically analyse the data and produce graphs.
- A single computer can monitor several patients simultaneously.
- It reduces the risk of nurses being exposed to contagious diseases.

Expert system medical diagnosis

The following stages show an example of how an expert system can be used to diagnose a patient's illness (similar logic could be used in other expert system examples):

- User of the expert system is asked a series of questions; each question asked takes into account the answers given in previous questions.
- The inference engine compares the entered data with data in the knowledge base, looking for possible matches.
- The rules base plays a key role in the matching process.
- Once a match is found, the system is able to suggest possible ailments.
- Possible solutions or advice can be given.
- The explanation system will explain how the expert system arrived at its conclusions.
- The user will see the output on a screen in the form of text or graphic images of the human anatomy, suggesting what and where the problem might be.
- The percentage probability of suggestions being correct is also given.
- The user can also request further information from the expert system to help in treatment.

Use of 3-D printers in medicine

3-D printers can produce working solid objects made in a variety of materials. They are being used successfully in medicine in the following areas:

- The creation of blood vessels and major arteries
- Used in surgical procedures to find out exactly what needs to be done before the actual surgery is carried out
- Can be used in patient consultations where exact models can be created to demonstrate the results of the surgical procedure
- Development of prosthetics (artificial limbs)
- Tissue engineering (bio-compatible materials and cells)
- Design and creation of new medical tools.

● Common errors

Questions on expert systems often cause problems due to a common error. If the question asks *how* an expert system is *used* to do a task, several candidates describe *how* an expert system is *created* – this would lose most, if not all, of the marks for the question. Be careful to read each question two or three times before answering.

Sample exam questions

a i Name four pieces of data sensors would collect in the monitoring of patients in a hospital.

ii Describe the output you would expect to see as part of the patient monitoring.

b Describe two methods for scanning patients to produce 3-D images which could allow the 3-D printing of organs.

Student's answer

a i Heart rate
   Body/blood temperature
   Blood pressure
   Oxygen levels in the blood.
ii Data in the form of digital printouts showing heartbeat, body
   temperature ...
   Beeping noises to indicate heart rate, and so on.
   Alarm if any measured parameter is out of range/tolerance.
   Moving graphs to show how blood pressure, and so on, is changing over time.
   Print outs of data and graphs for analysis by doctors/surgeons over a
   24-hour period.

Examiner's comments

a In part **ai**, other data such as respiration rate, brain activity or blood glucose levels could have been given. Be careful not to simply give temperature or pressure – the answer needs to refer to the patient, that is, the *body* temperature, *blood* pressure, and so on. In part **aii**, it is probably a good idea to mention three outputs:
  • Digital readouts on screen
  • Graphical readouts on screen
  • Printouts of data and graphs for later analysis.

Student's answer

b CT (computed tomography):
   produces images of internal parts of the body as a series of 0.1 mm thick
   'slices'
   MRI (magnetic resonance imaging):
   uses strong magnetic fields and radio waves to produce a series of images of
   internal body organs
   Data stored in the database (following one of the scanning methods) can
   later be sent to a 3-D printer to produce models of any of the organs.

Examiner's comments

b In this part, it is not necessary to go into any great depth; just give the basics of CT and MRI scans.

Examiner's tip

Where a list of four items is needed, don't exceed this; if there are any errors in the first four answers then marks would be lost since later answers would be ignored. For example, if you gave:

- respiration
- height of patient
- weight of patient
- heart rate
- blood glucose level
- body temperature

then only 2 marks would be awarded out of the possible four since answers 2 and 3 were incorrect and answers 5 and 6 would be ignored (even though correct!). Be careful!

● Library, stock control and recognition systems; tracking, GPS and GIS systems

Figure 6.7 Library book scanning system and GPS system

Library systems

Most library systems are now computer-controlled. They involve the use of barcodes on the books being borrowed and on the borrower's library card. The system allows books borrowed to be linked to a borrower automatically. Thus, it is now possible to send out reminders of overdue books automatically and to record other information such as the borrower's preferences, how many times a book has been taken out, and so on. Some systems now use RFID technology instead of barcodes.

Automatic stock control

Barcodes are used by supermarkets to allow automatic stock control to take place. The barcode on a product is scanned at the checkout and it is looked up on the stock file. Once it is found, the product price and product description is sent back to the checkout – this allows the calculation of the bill, and also produces an itemised bill. Each time an item is sold, the record (the key field of which is the barcode number) is updated to indicate the new stock level; this value is checked against a re-order level which allows the item to be reordered automatically if it equals or falls below this re-order level. When new stock arrives, the stock level of the item in the record is incremented.

EFTPOS is often used at the checkout till. When a customer pays electronically using their credit/debit card, an instruction is sent to the customer's bank to reduce their account by the amount of the bill. At the same time, an instruction is sent to the supermarket's bank to increase the account by an equal amount. No actual movement of money takes place.

Cambridge IGCSE ICT Study and Revision Guide © Graham Brown and David Watson, 2017

Automatic number plate recognition (ANPR) system

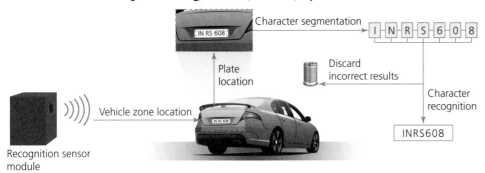

Figure 6.8 ANPR system

This system is used in car parks and as a security device to read the registration/number plate on a vehicle:

- The number plate is captured by a digital camera.
- The brightness and contrast of the number plate is adjusted so that all the characters can be read clearly.
- Afterwards, each character is segmented using software; OCR software is used to convert the characters into a string of editable text.
- This text string is then stored on a database.

Once the number plate is stored, it can be used to allow entry and exit to a car park or secure site as part of a car park charging system or security system.

Tracking system

RFID can be used for tracking (see Chapter 2). In conjunction with GPS, it can be used to track people:

- who are known criminal offenders
- who are elderly and need to be carefully monitored
- who are in a race, for example a marathon.

Internet cookies (small files of information created by websites and stored on your computer) can be used to monitor a person's internet activity, while key-logging is a technique used to track all entries made on a computer through its keyboard. These methods of tracking will be looked at in more detail in Chapter 8 Safety and Security.

Global positioning satellite (GPS) systems

GPS is used to determine the exact location of a vehicle or other form of transport (for example, an aeroplane).

Satellites orbiting the Earth transmit signals back to Earth. Microprocessors in GPS devices (known as *sat nav* in cars) pick up these signals and allow the GPS device to determine the exact position of the vehicle. In the case of sat nav, built-in maps are used to show the driver where they are on the road. Even more sophisticated systems know exactly where you are and can down shift an automatic gearbox on a car in readiness for a sharp bend or steep hill ahead. This has many other safety implications which you may like to consider (for example, prevention of accidents if the whereabouts of every car is known!).

GPS systems are safer since the driver doesn't have to consult maps, they allow for route re-planning if a road is closed, or can give useful information such as the nearest petrol station or café. They are not infallible; if the maps are out of date or the satellite signals are lost, the GPS can give incorrect instructions to the driver.

Geographic information systems (GIS)

This is a computer system that allows the user to map, model, query and analyse large amounts of data according to their location. It allows:

- the joining together of information on to a map
- carrying out calculations and presenting results in the form of a map, table and/or graphics
- engineers and scientists, for example, to see the information in different ways to determine patterns and relationships.

GIS is used by emergency services, environmentalists and teachers, for example.

Media communication systems

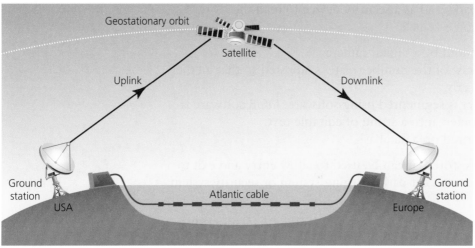

Figure 6.9 Global media communication system

Satellites allow data to be communicated around the world in a very short time. A typical satellite would contain:

- antennas (aerials to pick up data being sent to it from Earth)
- transponders (allow the receiving and sending of data)
- solar panels (to generate electricity to run on-board computers, and so on)
- propulsion unit (keeps the satellite in its correct orbit around the Earth).

Signals are beamed up to the satellite from a satellite dish on Earth and the signal is then boosted and transmitted back to the Earth. The frequency of the sending signals and receiving signals is different so that they don't become confused. This type of communication overcomes the curvature of the Earth and allows transmission over very large distances.

● Common errors

Many candidates don't fully understand how GPS systems work:

✖ GPS systems in cars send signals to satellites which then work out where they are and send this data back to the car.
✔ A satellite sends a signal to the GPS system in a car indicating where the satellite is in relation to the Earth. Software in the GPS device uses this information to work out where on the road the car is. Signals from three or four satellites are used to get a 3-D triangulation so that the exact position can be determined.

Sample exam questions

a Explain how ANPR can be used as a security system only allowing permitted cars to enter a secure site.

b Give three advantages and three disadvantages of using GPS as a form of navigation for the driver of a bus.

Student's answer

a Sensors at the entrance detect the presence of a vehicle and send a signal to the computer.
The computer instructs the digital camera to capture the number plate of the vehicle.
Software locates position of number plate on captured image and then adjusts brightness and contrast to ensure characters can be clearly read.
Each character is segmented and OCR software converts characters into a string of text.
The string of text is compared to stored number plate data held on a database.
If there is a match, the computer sends a signal to the barrier motor to raise the barrier.
A second sensor detects the rear of the vehicle and the barrier automatically drops again.

Examiner's comments

a This is a good answer from the candidate since it is tailored to the scenario in the question – a security system to check vehicles entering a secure site.

Student's answer

b Advantages:
Safer since there is no need to consult maps while on the move
Driver is warned of speed cameras and/or exceeding the speed limit
Driver is given key data such as proximity of petrol stations, restaurants, key tourist attractions, and so on.
Disadvantages:
If maps are not up to date, GPS can give incorrect instructions
Loss of satellite signals can cause problems
If incorrect start point or end point given, the system will give incorrect instructions.

Examiner's comments

b Here three different advantages and disadvantages have been given, which provides a good answer to the question; the candidate has given brief descriptions instead of simple statements.

Examiner's tip

Be careful not to make your answers too general. If a question gives a specific scenario, make sure your answer is modified to cover the scenario given.

Exam-style questions

1 a The perimeter around an airport is being monitored for sound levels
       and air pollution by the Environment Agency.

       Describe how sensors, data loggers/storage devices and computers
       could be used to monitor the perimeter environment. In your
       description, mention how the Environment Agency may use the
       collected data from the sensors.   [4 marks]

   b A car is fitted with sensors on the front bumper/fender. If the car gets
      too close to the vehicle in front of it, a warning is given and then the
      brakes are applied automatically. Sensor data is sent to an on-board
      microprocessor. This microprocessor can also pick up other data such as
      the speed of the car and whether the road is wet or dry.

      i   Name a suitable sensor to measure the distance.

      ii Explain how the microprocessor would work out if the car was too
          close to the vehicle in front of it.

      iii Describe how the sensors and microprocessor would be used
          to control the distance of the car from the vehicle in front
          of it.   [7 marks]

2 Copy the table and give suitable sensors for each of the following
   applications. A different sensor needs to be given in each case.   [6 marks]

Application	Suitable sensor
control water content in the soil in a greenhouse	
measure the quality of air in a building	
switch on the headlights of a car automatically when it gets dark	
automatically turn on the wiper blades of a car when it starts to rain	
pick up footsteps of an intruder in a building	
control the acidity levels in a chemical process	

3 Use the standard turtle graphics commands (see the Cambridge IGCSE
   ICT Coursebook) to draw the following shape. The measurements and the
   start and finish points are shown on the diagram.   [5 marks]

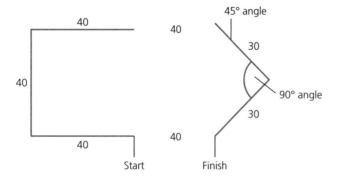

4 a Describe two ways a robot can be programmed to carry out a task such
       as spraying a car body with paint.   [4 marks]

   b The manufacturing company use expert systems to diagnose faults
      in the robots. Describe how an expert system would be set up to do
      this task.   [4 marks]

5 Describe how barcodes are used in an automatic stock control system in a supermarket. [5 marks]

6 a Give **two** advantages and **two** disadvantages of using GPS to navigate the driver of a car from town A to town B. [4 marks]

b Automatic number plate recognition (ANPR) systems go through a number of stages when the driver of a car approaches and leaves a car park.

The 12 stages are shown below, but they are not in the correct order. Copy and complete the table. Write the numbers 1 to 12 in the right-hand column to put each stage in its correct order. The first one has been done for you. [11 marks]

Stage description	Order
brightness and contrast of the number plate are adjusted so it can be read clearly	
on his return, the driver puts the car park ticket into the machine and pays for his parking	
sensors detect the car and send signals to the computer	1
each character on the number plate is recognised using OCR software	
sensors detect the rear of the car and the barrier is automatically dropped	
each character on the number plate is segmented	
using OCR software, the characters are converted into a string of editable text	
an algorithm is used to locate and isolate the number plate from the initial camera image	
the text string is stored on a database	
motorist drives to exit barrier and ANPR system recognises number plate and the barrier is automatically raised	
car park barrier is raised and the driver is issued with a car park ticket	
computer instructs the digital camera to capture an image of the front of the car	

Systems life cycle

The objectives of this chapter are to revise:

- analysis
- design

- development and testing
- implementation
- documentation
- evaluation.

● Key terms

Term	Definition
DFD	Data Flow Diagram
Validation	A process where the software checks that the data entered into it is reasonable.
Verification	A process that checks the accuracy of data entry or that data has not been corrupted during transmission.
Normal data	Data which is acceptable or reasonable which has an expected or known outcome.
Extreme data	Data which is at the limits of acceptability.
Abnormal data	Data which is outside the limits of acceptability and should be rejected by software.
Live data	Data which has actually been used in a real-life situation and has known outcomes.

● Analysis and design stages

Analysis stage

The analysis stage involves the following:

- Research or collect data from the current system in use.
- Establish inputs, outputs and processing done in the present system.
- Identify the main problems with the current system.
- Agree and interpret the objectives and requirements of the customers.
- Produce a cost–benefit analysis.
- Identify suitable hardware and software for the new system.
- Produce a data flow diagram (DFD) showing inputs, outputs and processing done.

The *feasibility study* is also a part of the analysis stage and involves the terms of reference, existing system overview, criteria and proposed solution (refer to the Cambridge IGCSE ICT Coursebook for full details of these four features).

When researching the current system, there are four common ways of carrying out *fact finding*:

Method used	Advantages	Disadvantages
Observation (this involves watching personnel using the existing system to see how it currently works)	• can give reliable and unbiased data • analyst gets a good overall view of the present system • a relatively inexpensive method	• people often work in a different way when they know they are being watched • because of the above reason, results can be skewed
Questionnaires (these are distributed to the workforce, managers or customers to find their views on the current system)	• relatively easy to complete and inexpensive to produce • individuals can remain anonymous • fast analysis if OMR used	• questionnaires are not very flexible • there is no immediate way to clarify a vague or incomplete answer to a question
Interviews (a one-to-one question-and-answer session either face to face or over the phone)	• questions asked can be modified based on interviewees' previous responses • interviewees tend to be more open • can delve more deeply into any areas where there are problems	• a very time-consuming and expensive method of collecting data • impossible for interviewees to be anonymous • interviewees may be hostile if they think their job is at risk

Method used	Advantages	Disadvantages
Existing paperwork (the analyst goes through existing paperwork, for example, operating instructions, training manuals, accounting system)	• allows the analyst to get a good idea of, for example, the memory requirements, type of input and output devices • information can be obtained which is not possible by any of the other methods	• a very time-consuming and expensive method of collecting data • the accuracy relies on whether the paperwork is up to date or used by the staff

Part of the analysis process involves the use of DFDs. These cover the input, output and processing done; identify problems with the current system; identify user and information requirements and identify system specifications. DFDs put the process into a logical diagrammatic form.

Design stage

The design stage is carried out after the analysis stage and includes:

- design of any data capture forms
- design screen layouts and output
- production of systems flowcharts
- design/choose the validation rules to be used
- design of the file structures
- production of algorithms and program flowcharts
- design of the testing strategy for the new system.

Data capture forms

These can be paper-based or online forms. The design of both types of form is very important since they must be easy to fill in.

Paper-based forms should use the following features:

- text boxes for address, and so on.
- character boxes with one character per box
- tick boxes wherever possible ☐ male ☐ female
- sufficient space given for answers
- a heading and very clear instructions on how to fill in the form
- a good colour scheme and a clear font.

Online forms should have the following features:

- character boxes (as shown above)
- on-screen help when completing the form
- dropdown/combo boxes where possible responses are limited
- radio buttons/tick boxes requiring a single click of a mouse
- automatic data validation on input data
- control buttons such as submit, next page, last page, and so on
- double entry boxes for confirmation, for example, when typing in email address.

Screen displays and printed reports

Screen outputs should be very clear and use as much of the screen as possible. Printed reports should clearly show all output fields and consider the need for headers and footers.

Systems flowcharts

These flowcharts use the standard symbols as shown on the right. They show how data flows through the system and how decisions are made. They are used to give an overall view of the proposed system. They don't

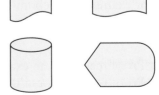

Cambridge IGCSE ICT Study and Revision Guide © Graham Brown and David Watson, 2017

form the basis of a program flowchart from which the programming code can be written, but they show the processes carried out and where various hardware devices are used in the system.

Verification

This is a way to check whether data entered or transmitted matches the original data. There are two common ways to carry out verification:

- Double entry: data is entered twice and it is then compared either after data entry or during data entry; this can be done by another human or, more commonly, by the computer (this method is often used when entering passwords or email addresses).
- Visual check: the person entering data compares it with the original document (for example, compares what is on the screen with the original printed document); this is *not* the same as proof reading!

Validation

This is the process where data is checked to see if it satisfies certain criteria when being input. Examples of validation include:

- Range check: this checks whether or not data lies between two end values.
- Look up check: this checks whether entered data exists in a stored table of data.
- Length check: this checks whether the entered data has the correct number of characters.
- Character/type check: this checks data is of the correct type, for example, text, numeric, and so on.
- Format/picture check: this checks data is in correct format, for example, date as dd/mm/yyyy.
- Presence check: this checks data is present in the field; it can't be left empty.
- Consistency check: this checks to see if data entered corresponds with another field, for example, if somebody types in 'Mr' in the Title field, they must also type in 'M' in the Sex field or an error will be flagged.
- Check digit: an extra digit added to a number which is generated by an algorithm; after transmission the same extra digit is recalculated to see if it matches the one sent.

File structures

When designing files it is important to consider field length, field name and data type. A data dictionary is used to show file structures, including any validation checks that may be carried out on the field data.

Testing strategy

A key part of the analysis and design stage; we will look at testing strategies in detail in the next section.

Common errors

It is common to confuse verification and validation; it is important to remember that verification doesn't check whether the data makes any sense (for example, somebody's height could be input as 1055 metres if that is the value on the original document – however, validation should trap this as a nonsensical value).

✖ Proof reading is an example of the use of verification.
✔ Proof reading doesn't check the data against the original document, so cannot be considered a form of verification.

Cambridge IGCSE ICT Study and Revision Guide © Graham Brown and David Watson, 2017

Sample exam questions

a   A shop sells books. A database is being set up to include: book title, author, ISBN (13-digit number), date published (for example, 23/11/2011), genre (for example, fiction), hardback or softback, and the price in dollars ($).

Copy and complete the following data dictionary for the database using suitable field names:

Field name	Field type	Suitable validation check
title	alphanumeric	none

a   Describe **two** ways of carrying out verification of data.

Student's answer

Field name	Field type	Suitable validation check
title	alphanumeric	none
author	text	character check
ISBN	integer (numeric)	length check
publication_date	alphanumeric	format check
genre	text	character check
hard_soft	Boolean/text	character check
price	real (currency)	range check

Examiner's comments

a   The candidate has chosen reasonable field names. Other field types could have been chosen, for example, ISBN could be alphanumeric if in the form: 978-1-471-89033-8. Other validation checks could also be used, for example, hard_soft could be a length check if H and S are the expected input values.

Student's answer

b   Double entry – data is entered twice and two sets of data are compared by two operators or by the computer (for example, entering a password twice). Visual check – entered data is compared to the original document (for example, screen input checked with paper document).

Examiner's comments

b   The candidate has given two reasonable descriptions together with examples. Giving examples is always a useful addition in case the definitions given are a little weak – the examples could just sway the examiner to give you the benefit of doubt and award the marks.

Examiner's tip

Field names can be anything really provided they tie up with the kind of data, for example, field name of 'example' to represent type of weather would be regarded as *too* vague to be of any use.

● Development, testing, implementation, documentation and evaluation

Development

Once analysis and design is completed it is necessary to develop the new system. For example, a database requires finalisation of file structures, validation/verification routines need to be finalised and the user interface needs to be fully developed.

Testing strategies

Modular programming is often adopted (here the entire program is broken up into parts). Each module needs to be fully tested. Once this is done, the whole program needs to be fully tested again to make sure none of the modules conflict. Data used in testing falls into four categories:

- Normal: data which is acceptable or reasonable, which will give a known outcome.
- Abnormal: data which is outside the limits of acceptability and should be rejected by the software.
- Extreme: this is data at the limits of acceptability.
- Live data: data which has actually been used in real life, which will produce known outcomes; the actual outcomes from the new system will be compared to outcomes from the existing system using the same data.

For example, an online form asks somebody to type in their age. The acceptable range will be 5 to 140. The following examples show each type of validation check:

- Normal: 22, 58, 74
- Abnormal: –2, 221, fifty-six
- Extreme: 5 or 140 (end values).

Implementation

Once a new system is fully tested it needs to be implemented. Four common methods of implementation exist:

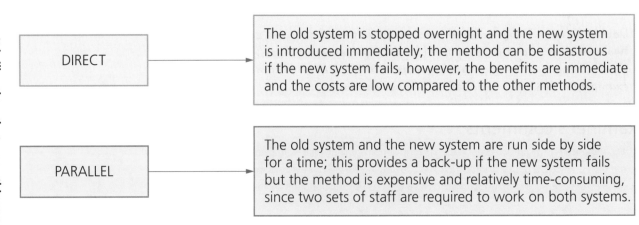

| DIRECT | The old system is stopped overnight and the new system is introduced immediately; the method can be disastrous if the new system fails, however, the benefits are immediate and the costs are low compared to the other methods. |

| PARALLEL | The old system and the new system are run side by side for a time; this provides a back-up if the new system fails but the method is expensive and relatively time-consuming, since two sets of staff are required to work on both systems. |

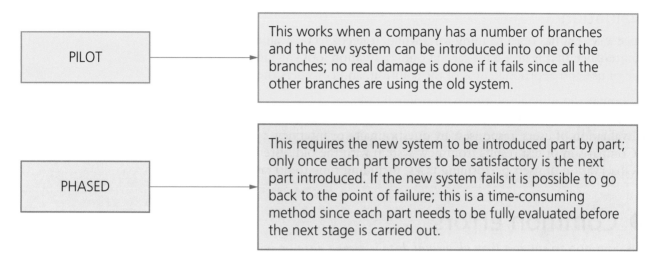

Documentation

Two main types of documentation will be supplied with the new system once it is implemented – user documentation and technical documentation. User documentation is developed to help the end user understand how to use the new system. It will include examples of input and output, the meaning of possible error messages and how to carry out certain tasks such as printing or updating files. Technical documentation is designed to help a systems analyst and/or programmer update the system sometime in the future or help in troubleshooting if any problems occur. The following shows typical examples of the contents of both types of documentation:

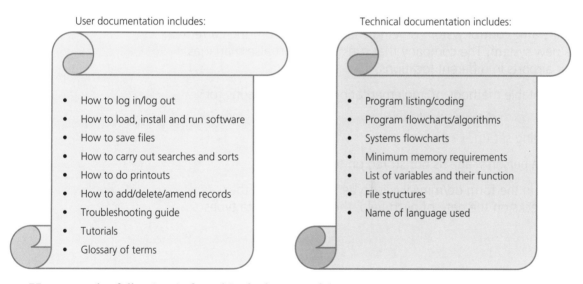

However, the following is found in *both* types of documentation:

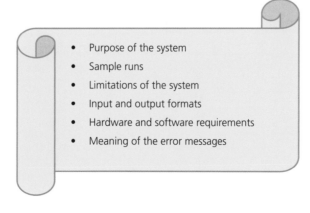

Evaluation

Once a system has been running for a while, it needs to be evaluated and any maintenance that is necessary carried out. Evaluation looks at the efficiency, ease of use and appropriateness of the solution, and considers the following:

- Comparison of final solution with original task.
- Identification of any limitations and any necessary improvements.
- Evaluation of users' responses (by questionnaire or interview).
- Comparison of test results from new system with the old system.
- Observation of users performing tasks, including time to do tasks.

● Common errors

It is common to suggest that *abnormal data* is *wrong data* or *incorrect data*. No data is incorrect or wrong – data can only be outside a given set of criteria.

It is also common to suggest 'Direct implementation is carried out directly' or 'Direct implementation completely replaces the old system'. The first statement uses the term 'directly' which isn't giving a description and is merely repeating the wording of the term itself. The second statement is not unique to direct implementation – all methods of implementation replace the whole system at some point; the advantage of the direct method is that its benefits are available immediately.

Sample exam questions

a An airport air traffic control system is being changed over from the current system to a new system. The company that runs the airport also manages another four airports in different locations.

Describe two suitable methods of implementation and give reasons for your choice.

b A database is being set up.

 i Explain why a person's 'age' is not stored on the database.

 ii Date of birth in the form dd/mm/yyyy is to be stored. To test the validation checks on the date of birth field, the following data types are input:

 normal

 abnormal

 extreme.

 Give examples of each type of data when applied to the *month* part of the field.

Student's answer

a Direct — old air traffic control system stopped overnight and the new system implemented immediately.
Pilot — one of the airports uses the new system for a period to see if it functions correctly; if everything checks out, the system will be rolled out to the other airports.
Neither method employs parallel systems or partially changed systems for safety reasons; pilot changeover is the most risky of the two examples given if there are any faults.

Examiner's comments

a The student correctly identified that parallel and phased would not be acceptable methods. They also gave some misgivings about using the pilot method. This is a good sound answer at the grade 'A' level.

Student's answer

b i Age will change every year, so the database would need to be manually updated every year for each person on their birthday.
   ii Normal: 4 or 6 or ...
       Abnormal: −5 or 15 or ...
       Extreme: 1 or 12

Examiner's comments

b The student could have given any 'normal' value between 1 and 12. They gave two examples because of the potential ambiguous wording of the question. The two 'abnormal' values of −5 and 15 were okay, any value < 1 or > 12 would have been acceptable. It would also be acceptable to give a non-numeric value. There are only two possible answers for 'extreme' data and these were correctly identified.

> **Examiner's tip**
> This question stated 'Give examples ...'. It is unclear whether the plural refers to the fact that there are three types of data or whether more than one example for each data type is needed. When confronted with a question which is not entirely clear to you, always err on the side of caution and consider the possible meanings of the question when answering it.

Exam-style questions

1 A car manufacturing company has decided to bring in a systems analyst to upgrade the current system.

   a Describe **three** ways that could be used to do *fact finding* so that the current system can be assessed. Give a disadvantage of each named method. [6 marks]

   b Copy the table. Tick (✓) the appropriate column to indicate whether each item is part of the analysis stage or the design stage. [6 marks]

Item	Analysis	Design
identify suitable hardware and software		
create file structures		
produce data flow diagrams		

Cambridge IGCSE ICT Study and Revision Guide © Graham Brown and David Watson, 2017

Item	Analysis	Design
produce a cost–benefit report		
research current system		
production of algorithms and program flowcharts		

c One of the new features is an online form to order so that customers can choose and order their new car directly. Design an online form which allows input of: *customer name, dealer where car is delivered, model of car, colour of car, manual or automatic, desired delivery date* and the ability to move to another page to choose from the options list. [6 marks]

2 a A company sells books online. Customers complete a form when ordering and the information input is stored in an order database. The database includes:

- date of birth (in the form dd/mm/yyyy)
- person's title (Mr, Mrs, Ms, Miss or Dr)
- gender (M or F)
- order number (in the form AANNNNNNA where A = letter and N = digit)
- number of items bought (maximum of 50 items)
- customer's email address.

Write down a validation check for each of the six inputs. A different validation check should be given in each case. [6 marks]

b i A password needs to be used each time a customer logs in to make an order. Describe a suitable verification check. [2 marks]

ii The number of items ordered can be any whole number between 1 and 50. Give examples of normal, abnormal and extreme data to test the 'number of items bought' field. [3 marks]

3 A new system needs to be implemented. Describe **three** implementation methods and give an advantage and a disadvantage of each of the three named methods. [9 marks]

4 Documentation is supplied with the new system. Eight items are listed in the following table. Copy the table. Tick (✓) the appropriate box to show whether each items is in the user documentation, technical documentation or in both. [8 marks]

Item	User documentation	Technical documentation	Both types of documentation
how to sort and search			
tutorials and FAQs			
sample runs and test results			
minimum memory requirements			
hardware/software requirements			
how to add/delete/amend records			
systems flowcharts			
meaning of error messages			

Cambridge IGCSE ICT Study and Revision Guide © Graham Brown and David Watson, 2017

Safety and security

● Key terms

Term	Definition
E-safety	Keeping personal data safe when using a device connected to the internet.
SSL	Secure Socket Layer
TLS	Transport Layer Security
Firewall	Hardware or software that sits between a user's computer and an external network, which filters data coming to and from the computer.
Cypher script/text	Result of putting plain text through an encryption process.
Plain text	Original message before going through an encryption process.
Web beacons	Graphic image linked to an external web server that is placed into an html-formatted message; can be used to verify that an email address is valid when the message is opened.
Digital certificate	Pair of files stored on user's computer; each pair contains a public key and private key.
Encryption	Process in which data appears meaningless without the use of the correct decryption key.
Spam	A form of junk or unsolicited mail sent over the internet to a recipient on an email mailing list.
Cookies	Small files or code stored on a user's computer; they are effectively a small look-up table containing linked pairs of key data values.
Hypervisor	Software, firmware or hardware that creates and runs a virtual machine.

● Physical safety and security of data

Physical safety

This covers health risks (for example, back/neck pain, RSI, eyestrain/headaches and ozone irritation) and safety risks (for example, electrocution, trip hazards and fire risks). It is important to understand exactly what can cause all these risks and how they can be eliminated or minimised.

For example:

Health risks, such as RSI, are caused by excessive typing on a keyboard or clicking a mouse button; these can be eliminated or minimised by taking regular breaks or by using ergonomic keyboards or cushioned mouse mats. Safety risks, such as a tripping wire hazard, can be removed by using trunking or using wireless devices wherever possible. There are many more examples which are covered at great length in the Cambridge IGCSE ICT Coursebook.

E-safety

This refers to keeping personal data safe when using any device connected to the internet. Personal data includes: name, address, date of birth, medical history and banking details. However, some personal data is referred to as being *sensitive*: ethnic origin, political views, religion, sexual orientation and criminal activity.

E-safety refers to:

- not giving out personal data (including photos) to people you don't know
- maintaining the privacy settings on devices connected to the internet
- only using trusted websites or ones which have been recommended
- only opening emails from, and sending emails to, known sources and making use of spam boxes
- taking great care when using social networking sites and online games.

Security of data

This includes: hacking, phishing/smishing/vishing, pharming, spyware, viruses, spam, cookies and moderated/unmoderated forums.

■ **Hacking:** this is the act of gaining unauthorised access to devices.
This can lead to identity theft, loss of data and illegal use of personal data. The risk can be minimised by using firewalls, passwords and user ids.

■ **Phishing:** the creator sends out legitimate-looking emails to target users; as soon as any link in the email or attachment is clicked on, the user is sent to a fake website; they could also be asked to respond to an email claiming 'You have just purchased a book for $25.95 – if this is not you please click on one of the links below'.
This can lead to identity fraud and users can be tricked into giving personal data (such as bank details) when the user goes to the fake website or responds to the email.
Many ISPs filter out phishing attacks, but users need to be cautious when receiving emails from unknown sources.
Note: also recall associated risks known as smishing (SMS phishing) and vishing (voice mail phishing).

■ **Pharming:** this is malicious code installed on a user's computer or on a web server; this code re-directs the user to a fake website without their knowledge.
This can lead to identity fraud and users can be tricked into giving personal data (such as bank details) when the user goes to the fake website.
Some anti-spyware can detect pharming code; users should never copy and paste web addresses into the URL window.

■ **Spyware:** this is software that gathers data by monitoring key presses on a user's computer keyboard; the gathered data is sent back to the person who sent the spyware in the first place (also known as key logging software).
Spyware gives the originator access to all data entered by the keyboard; spyware can also install other spyware, read cookie data and change the user's default settings.
Using anti-spyware software should help; use dropdown boxes when entering data wherever possible or use a touch screen.

■ **Viruses:** this is program code/software that can replicate itself with the intention of deleting or corrupting files on the computer.
Corrupted files can cause the computer to malfunction (such as crash or run slow); important files can be deleted or modified to alter how software works on the computer (potential security risk).
Use anti-virus software, which should be kept up to date and run in the background at all times; also don't open software or emails from unknown sources.

■ **Spam:** this is unsolicited email sent over the internet to a recipient on a mailing list.
Spam can 'clog up' a user's inbox with unwanted emails; it can also lead to phishing attacks.

Cambridge IGCSE ICT Study and Revision Guide © Graham Brown and David Watson, 2017

Set up ISP to filter out spam and delete the mail immediately; block images in html messages that spammers use as web beacons.

■ **Cookies:** these are small files/code stored on a user's computer; they are effectively small look-up tables that contain pairs of values.
Cookies are used to remember user's preferences each time they visit websites.
Cookies form anonymous user profiles and don't contain personal data such as passwords or credit/debit card numbers and don't pose a security risk in that sense; however, it is a good idea to remove cookies from internet settings unless you visit the website on a regular basis.

Forums: these are termed 'moderated' and 'unmoderated'. Moderated forums are online discussion groups in which all the posts are checked by an administrator before they are allowed to be posted. The internet is an unmoderated forum since no one 'owns' it; the only safeguards are voluntary sets of rules and protocols.

Note 1: A user can usually tell if they are connected to a secure website by the use of a green banner containing the web page/website name. The use of a green padlock and the use of https instead of just http are often used to identify a secure website (see protocols below):

Note 2: Some of the security risks above refer to online fraud. If a customer uses their credit card on line there a number of ways they can encounter fraud:

● The website being visited is fake (see Security of data above) which means a fraudster can gain key information from the customer without their knowledge.
● The user's computer or the website has been hacked, meaning important data can be accessed (such as credit card data, PINs, and so on); this can also be caused by certain viruses.
● Installation of spyware on a user's computer can relay back all key presses to a hacker.
● The user can be tricked by fraudsters sending out fake emails such as:

Once the user clicks on the link, they will be asked for passwords, credit card numbers and so on – there are many clues this is a fraud (for example, the beginning 'Dear User' would never be used, reputable companies will already have your card details, and so on).

● Common errors

It is very common to see confusion between phishing and pharming (and also incorrect spellings – most notably fishing and farming!).

Sample exam questions

a   Name **three** examples of physical safety risks when using computers. In each case, describe a way to remove or minimise the named risk.

b   Describe two differences between phishing and pharming.

Student's answer

a *Electrocution: use an RCB (residual circuit breaker); make sure all wires are properly insulated; don't take drinks into the computer room.*
   Trip hazard: use cable ducts to make trailing wires safe; cover wires or have them tucked away safely; use wireless (Wi-Fi) connections wherever possible.
   Fire risk: have a CO2/dry powder fire extinguisher in every room; don't cover vents on computer monitors; don't overload wall sockets; change to low voltage hardware wherever possible.

Examiner's comments

a The candidate has given more than one way to remove or mitigate the risks; this is probably more than is required to gain full marks for the question. It is essential that the named method of mitigation matches up to the risk.

Student's answer

b *Phishing requires an email to be sent.*
   Phishing requires the user to take some action (for example, click on a link).
   Pharming requires code to be stored on a user's computer or web server.

Examiner's comments

b The candidate has given three good differences between the two terms.

Examiner's tip

When asked to describe the differences between two (or more) terms, don't give opposites as one of your answers, for example, *'Phishing requires emails to be sent but pharming doesn't require any emails to be sent out'*.

This counts as one point only. Distinct differences must be given to gain the marks.

● Firewalls, protocols, encryption, authentication and cloud security

Firewalls

These are either hardware or software that sit between a user's computer and an external network. They filter data coming in and data going out of a user's computer. The tasks of a firewall can be summarised as:

- Examine traffic between computer and a network.
- Check incoming/outgoing data meets certain criteria; if it doesn't, user is warned and data flow blocked.
- Keep a log of daily traffic.
- Keep a list of IP addresses thus preventing access to certain websites.
- Help prevent viruses and hacking.

Protocols

There are two common protocols which are used when a computer wishes to communicate across a network: SSL (secure socket layer) and TLS (transport layer security).

SSL – when a user logs on to a website, SSL encrypts the data; the user will know if SSL is being applied due to https or the green padlock appearing; it involves a communication between the web browser on the user's computer and the website.

TLS – this is similar to SSL but is more modern and more effective; it uses two layers known as the 'record protocol' (which contains the data being transferred) and the 'handshake protocol' (which permits website and user to authenticate each other).

The basic differences between SSL and TLS are that TLS can be extended by adding new authentication methods, TLS can make use of 'session caching' and TLS separates the two protocol layers.

Encryption

This makes data unreadable unless the user has the correct decryption key. The original message (called 'plain text') is put through an encryption algorithm (using the encryption key) and it produces the encrypted message (known as 'cypher script/text'). If a hacker breaks into a computer system, they can certainly delete, copy or corrupt the data but they won't be able to understand it.

Authentication

This is used to verify that data comes from a secure and trusted source. It uses digital certificates, passwords and biometrics as part of the authentication process.

Digital certificate
This is a pair of files which consist of a public key (known to everyone) and a private key (known to a selected group only). For example, when an email is sent, it is more secure if digital certification is added. The recipient can check it comes from a trusted source by viewing the public key information – this consists of: the sender's email address, name of the digital certificate owner, a serial number, expiry date, public key and digital signature of the certificate authority (CA).

Passwords and user ids
Passwords should always be strong and changed frequently. It is common practice for a strong password to contain: upper and lower case letters, digits and other keyboard characters, for example, FX43ab*!/8. When logging into most systems, a user will be asked to give a user id *and* a password. The user id and password will be stored as a linked pair on the system – if they don't match up then access will be denied.

The user id is often a person's email address and is usually something linked to the application being used. Usually a user id is unique form of identification. When the password is typed in it is shown as ********** to prevent anybody accidentally using it. It is often necessary to type in the password twice (this is called verification). This is to confirm no typing errors were made.

Biometrics

These make use of certain unique characteristics of human beings. They include:

- fingerprint scans
- signature recognition
- retina scans
- iris recognition
- face recognition
- voice recognition.

They all have a range of advantages and disadvantages:

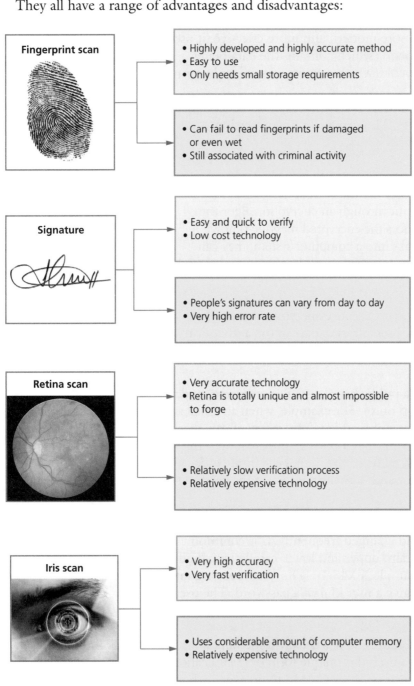

| Fingerprint scan | • Highly developed and highly accurate method
• Easy to use
• Only needs small storage requirements |
| | • Can fail to read fingerprints if damaged or even wet
• Still associated with criminal activity |

| Signature | • Easy and quick to verify
• Low cost technology |
| | • People's signatures can vary from day to day
• Very high error rate |

| Retina scan | • Very accurate technology
• Retina is totally unique and almost impossible to forge |
| | • Relatively slow verification process
• Relatively expensive technology |

| Iris scan | • Very high accuracy
• Very fast verification |
| | • Uses considerable amount of computer memory
• Relatively expensive technology |

Enter User ID & Password

Enter User ID & Password

Enter User ID: group_userid

Enter Password: ***********

OK   Cancel

Cambridge IGCSE ICT Study and Revision Guide © Graham Brown and David Watson, 2017

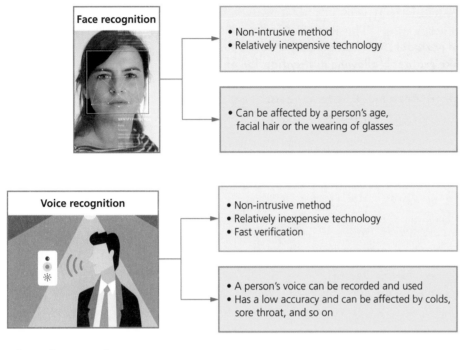

Cloud security

The advantages of storing data on the 'cloud' can be summarised as follows:

- No need to buy and carry memory devices around with you
- Files will always be backed up at the end of each day
- It is possible to synchronise devices so that available files are always the most up to date
- Allows for collaborative storage.

The main security issues are:

- Is there adequate security of building where storage devices are kept?
- Is there good resistance to natural and man-made disasters (fire, flood, power cuts, and so on)?
- Are the staff overseeing the storage devices trustworthy?
- Are there adequate provisions against hacking, viruses and pharming?

● Common errors

It is very common to see candidates become confused regarding the role of firewalls.

✖ When installed on a computer, a firewall will always prevent hacking and viruses.

✔ When installed on a computer a firewall will warn a user of possible hacking and virus dangers, but it cannot be assumed that it will filter out all possible risks.

Sample exam questions

a Explain **three** differences between SSL and TLS.

b Describe **three** advantages of using cloud storage to store files.

Cambridge IGCSE ICT Study and Revision Guide © Graham Brown and David Watson, 2017

Student's answer

a *TLS uses two layers; the record protocol (which contains the data being transferred) and the handshake protocol (allowing authentication of website and user's computer).*
TLS uses session caching, which creates a much faster process.
The handshaking and record protocols are separated processes.

Examiner's comments

a The candidate has given a very reasonable answer but further expansion on session caching and what is meant by separating the two layers would be a welcome addition.

Student's answer

b *No need to carry memory devices around with you.*
No need to buy expensive memory/storage devices.
The files will always be backed up each day.

Examiner's comments

b Other advantages such as ability to synchronise devices and ability to allow for collaborative storage would have been equally correct.

Examiner's tip
In questions where an explanation is asked for, it is often a good idea to expand your points slightly within the bounds of the space provided on the answer paper. A good explanation or examples could cover a weak description and allow you to recover lost marks.

Exam-style questions

1 Which items are being described below:

   a Process in which data appears meaningless without the appropriate 'unlocking' key

   b Code stored on a user's computer which is effectively a small look-up table containing linking pairs of key data

   c Original message before it goes through an encryption process

   d Unsolicited emails sent over the internet to a recipient on a mailing list which 'clog up' their inbox

   e Hardware and software that sit between a user's computer and an external network which filters data coming in and out of the computer

   f Keeping personal data safe when using any device connected to the internet. [6 marks]

2 Three computer security risks include:

- spyware

- phishing

- hacking.

Explain the meaning of each security risk and why it is a security risk. In each case, give one way of mitigating or removing the risk. [9 marks]

Audiences

Key terms

Term	Definition
Software piracy	Making and distributing illegal copies of software.
Product key	Unique string of characters which is supplied with software to indicate it comes from a genuine source.
Dongle	Device which connects to a computer through the USB port – it allows wireless communication with devices or stores key files to allow software to run on that computer only.
FAST	Federation Against Software Theft

Audiences, software copyright, impact of ICT solutions and policing the internet

Audiences

When using ICT to present information, it is important to consider the audience as not all solutions will be appropriate, or relevant, depending on the audience that you are addressing. The following factors should be taken into consideration:

- Age, experience and knowledge of the audience
- Audience expectations
- Language used
- Whether multimedia and interactive interface should be used
- Length of the presentation
- Which examples would be helpful and/or appropriate.

Software copyright and piracy

Software is protected by the usual copyright laws. However, to further reduce the risk of piracy, the following measures are taken:

- Use of a product key supplied with original software
- Sign a licence agreement
- Use of holograms on original packaging
- Use of dongles to prevent illegal use.

Impact of ICT solutions

Legal: this covers the law; whether an action is punishable by law, for example, illegal copying and distribution of software.

Morality: this governs private and personal interactions between people; the human desire to distinguish between right and wrong.

Ethics: this governs professional interaction, that is, codes of behaviour; it is often illegal, or it may just be an act carried out which is regarded as breaking a code of conduct.

Cultural: this refers to the attitudes, values and practices shared by a society; this will change from culture to culture.

Policing the internet

Policing of the internet was covered in detail in Chapter 4, please refer to that section.

● Common errors

It is very common to see the terms copyright and software piracy confused:

✖ Copyright protection makes it much harder for software to be pirated.
✔ Copyright laws make the pirating of software illegal; however, they do not actively prevent the piracy from taking place.

Sample exam questions

a Explain why the following need to be carefully considered when producing and giving a presentation:

language

age

examples.

b Give **three** rules which govern the copyright of software.

Student's answer

a Language:
language should not be 'colourful' to avoid offending the audience
technical terms should not be used if the audience is very young and/or inexperienced.
Age:
young people will respond in a different way from older people
young people like less 'writing' and 'talking' and prefer more visual effect
young people have different experiences and expectations compared to a more mature audience
young people respond better to multimedia elements.
Examples:
examples must be chosen so that they don't offend certain audience attendees
examples used should relate to the experiences and age of the audience.

Examiner's comments

a The candidate has correctly given as many examples as possible to illustrate the three aspects given in the question.

Cambridge IGCSE ICT Study and Revision Guide © Graham Brown and David Watson, 2017

Student's answer

b Don't make copies and distribute them without permission.
Don't plagiarise coding from software and use it in your own software claiming you wrote it yourself.
Don't use the name of copyrighted material on your own material/software without gaining permission first.

Examiner's comments

b Three different copyright rules were correctly given here.

Exam-style questions

1 Use the following terms to complete the five statements that follow (four of the terms will not be used).

copyright ethics product key culture legal software piracy encryption morality virus

a A unique string of characters which is supplied with software to indicate it comes from a genuine source is known as:

b Illegal copying and distributing of software without the owner's permission is known as:

c This term governs private and personal interactions between people; it is the human desire to distinguish between right and wrong.

d This governs professional interaction in codes of behaviour such as some action carried out which is regarded as breaking a code of conduct.

e This term refers to the attitude, values and practices shared by a society. [5 marks]

2 a When producing a presentation, describe **four** things to consider regarding the potential audience. [4 marks]

b The people giving the presentation hand out some software to the audience. Explain how the audience will know this software is genuine and not illegal copies. [3 marks]

c Describe the ways in which software is protected from piracy. [3 marks]

Communication

Key objectives

The objectives of this chapter are to revise:

- communication restraints when using emails
- email groups
- cloud storage
- spam

- the internet
- intranets
- the world wide web (www)
- blogs, wikis and social networking sites
- search engines.

● Key terms

Term	Definition
Netiquette	InterNET etIQUETTE which refers to the need to respect others' views and display common courtesy.
Spam	Unsolicited emails sent out to users in an email group.
Intranet	Computer network based on internet technology but designed to meet the internal needs for sharing information/data within a single organisation/company.
Extranet	Part of a company's intranet which is extended to users outside the company or organisation; although it allows access to internal data by external users, all extranet communications are encrypted over a VPN which makes it more secure than the internet.
Data redundancy	Same data stored on more than one device (for example, a server) in case of maintenance, repair or potential data loss.
Public cloud	Storage environment where the customer/client and provider are different companies.
Private cloud	Storage provided by a dedicated environment behind a firewall; the customer/client and provider are integrated and operate as a single entity.
Hybrid cloud	This is a mixture of public and private cloud storage, where some data resides on the private cloud and some on the public cloud.
http	HyperText Transfer Protocol
URL	Uniform Resource Locator
ftp	File Transfer Protocol
ISP	Internet Service Provider
Blog	weB LOG
VPN	Virtual Private Network
Search engine	Software that allows the user to search for information on the internet using key words/phrases and sophisticated algorithms.
Hit	Number of occasions where key words/phrases typed in match with websites/web pages.

Cambridge IGCSE ICT Study and Revision Guide © Graham Brown and David Watson, 2017

Emails, spam, internet, intranets and cloud storage

 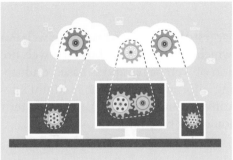

Figure 10.1 Emailing and cloud storage

Emails

Most countries have laws to protect people against email misuse. Some of the safeguards include:

- Commercial email senders must have an opt-out or unsubscribe feature.
- Email subject lines must not be misleading.
- Valid contact details must be included in commercial emails.
- Many countries don't allow email groups to be set up by 'trawling' companies that already hold email addresses.
- Language used in emails must be of an acceptable nature.

It is important that emails follow all copyright regulations and that users are advised to use passwords to secure email addresses and inboxes.

'Netiquette' is an important aspect of any material posted or transmitted on the internet. There are numerous resources regarding what constitutes netiquette but the following summarises many of the common rules:

- No abusive language, and messages should be clear.
- Posts can be read by general public; therefore, spelling, grammar and privacy must be considered.
- Don't use capital letters except where necessary and keep emoticons to a minimum.

Email groups

Email groups are used for a number of purposes:

- It is easier for a user to send out multiple emails if the addresses are all grouped together under a single name; the user then just has to use that single name in the 'To' box.
- Companies and organisations can group people together for marketing purposes, for example, according to age, ethnicity, hobbies, favourite music, and so on. This means that each email can target specific groups.
- 'Spammers' can create email groups by buying addresses of people from certain companies or from software that 'raids' address books on computers or email companies – this means that several thousand people can be sent spam by simply pressing the <Enter> key.
- Companies use email groups to set up meetings (for example, for a video conference) to ensure everybody is always invited to attend – it would be easy to omit a person if the email addresses were all typed in individually; this way you can be sure all the correct recipients are sent messages.

Spam

This topic was covered in Chapter 8. Please refer back to that section to refresh your memory.

The internet

The internet is the world's largest WAN. The world wide web (www or web) is only *part* of the internet which can be accessed using a web browser. It consists of a massive collection of web pages and is based on http. The world wide web is a way of accessing information over the medium known as the internet (which consists of software and hardware) – the two terms 'www' and 'internet', therefore, should not be confused.

Intranets

An intranet is a network which meets the needs of a company or organisation to enable the sharing of information/data. Intranets are not available for access by the general public. Since many intranets are internal, they are generally more secure than the internet. Information available can also be specific to the company only and it is possible to control external links (for example, the internet).

'Extranets' allow intranets to be accessed/extended outside the organisation, for example, to gain access over a mobile phone or via a VPN (using the internet). There are many safeguards to protect the network and allow only certain users to have access to the secure servers. This will include passwords and encryption which makes it more secure than the internet.

There are key differences between the internet and intranets:

- The internet contains global and public data/information whereas intranets have data/information specific to the company.
- To access an intranet requires a user id and password and it can only be accessed from agreed computers within the organisation (or from valid extranet users).
- The internet can be accessed by anyone from anywhere in the world.
- The internet has public access; the intranet is private access only.

Cloud storage

Cloud storage is a method of data storage where the data is stored on offsite servers and users pay a subscription each month to have their data stored on these servers. Usually data is stored on more than one server (to allow maintenance, repair and back-up) – this is known as 'data redundancy'.

There are three common types of cloud storage:

Public cloud – the customer/client and cloud storage provider are different companies.

Private cloud – the storage is provided by a dedicated environment where the client/customer and cloud storage provider are integrated and operate as a single entity accessible by that company only.

Hybrid cloud – this is a combination of the two types of cloud storage described above; some data resides on the public cloud (for example, data which is less sensitive) and some on the private cloud (for example, data which needs to be kept out of the public access).

Cambridge IGCSE ICT Study and Revision Guide © Graham Brown and David Watson, 2017

Having data stored on cloud storage facilities allows the following positive features:

- Data on the cloud can be accessed from any device at any time, from anywhere in the world where there is internet access.
- There is no need to buy and carry around portable storage devices; data is also automatically backed up each day.
- All devices can be synchronised so that the data is always up to date and the same on every device.
- The storage capacity is almost unlimited.

But of course there are also negative features:

- There are security issues of data, which is a major issue for many people; it is possible for data to be hacked and sent out over the public highway.
- It is necessary to always have a good internet connection.
- Storage costs can be high (including internet costs).
- It is possible for the cloud storage provider to go out of business, which would cause uncertainty.

● Common errors

It is very common to see confusion between the terms 'www' and 'the internet'; the two need to be regarded as separate entities.

Sample exam questions

a Give **three** reasons why email groups are set up.

b Explain the difference between passive and active attacks on emails.

Student's answer

a It is easier to send out multiple emails if all email addresses are grouped together under a single name.

Companies/organisations can group people together for marketing purposes, for example, by age, gender, interests, and so on.

Companies can use email groups to set up meetings (for example, video conferencing) — it would be easy to omit somebody if all email addresses had to be typed in individually.

Examiner's comments

a The three reasons given are all different; this is important to ensure access to the maximum marks allocated to the question.

Student's answer

b Passive: involves release of email material to other users without your consent.
Active: involves modification of user's messages or even denial of service; this can involve viruses or phishing attacks.

Examiner's comments

b Although the answer given would score high marks, it may have been better to set it out as an 'essay' rather than use bullet points since the question asked for an explanation to be given highlighting the differences.

Examiner's tip

If bullet points are used when answering a question which asks for an explanation or description of differences, it is often a good idea to also give a short paragraph summarising the differences highlighted in the bullet points.

● General internet terms and search engines

Hypertext transfer protocol

Hypertext transfer protocol (http) is a set of rules that must be obeyed when transferring data across the internet. Protocols are sets of rules agreed by the 'sender' and 'recipient' when data is being transferred between devices. When a web page is being accessed, entering http:// at the front of an address tells the web browser that http rules for communication are to be obeyed.

If http is omitted from the address, most web browsers now default to http.

When some form of security (for example, SSL or TLS) certification or encryption is used (see Chapter 8) then the protocol is changed to https (this is often seen as the padlock symbol 🔒). The letter 's' after http refers to secure.

Because of encryption, it is slower to use https than http, so it is usually only adopted when sensitive or private data is being transferred across the internet.

Web browsers

A web browser is software which allows a user to display a web page on their computer screen. It interprets or translates the HTML (hypertext mark-up language – see later chapters) from websites and shows the result of the translation. This can often be in the form of videos, images or sound. Most web browsers share the following features:

- They have a home page.
- They have the ability to store a user's favourite websites/pages.

Cambridge IGCSE ICT Study and Revision Guide © Graham Brown and David Watson, 2017

- They keep a history of the websites visited by the user.
- They give the ability to go backward and forward to websites opened.
- They have *hyperlinks* to allow users to navigate between web pages; these hyperlinks are shown as blue_underlined_text or use a small picture, such as a pointed finger 👆, under a phrase or image. By clicking on a hyperlink the user is sent to another website or web page.

Web browsers use **uniform resource locators** (URLs) to access websites, retrieve files, and so on. They are represented by a set of four numbers, for example, 109.108.158.1 (http://109.108.158.1).

File transfer protocol
File transfer protocol (ftp) is a network protocol used when transferring files from one computer to another over the internet. The main differences between ftp and http include:

- http is used to access the world wide web (www).
- ftp is used to download data from file servers, whereas http is used to download data from web servers.
- ftp files are transferred from one device to another and copied into memory.
- http transfers the contents of web pages into a web browser for viewing.
- ftp upload is used for large files; http tends to be used to upload smaller files.

Internet Service Provider
An internet service provider (ISP) is a company that provides users with access to the internet. When a user registers with an ISP, an account is set up and they are given log in details such as user id and password.

Blogs, wikis and social networking sites

Figure 10.2 Social networking and blogging

Blogs
These are personal internet journals where the author (blogger) will type in their observations on a given topic for others to read; this may involve links to other websites. Anyone can read blogs, but only the blogger can change the contents. Entries are organised from most recent to least recent. Associated with blogs are 'microblogs' and 'b-blogs'.

Wikis
These are web applications or websites that allow users to create and edit web pages using any web browser. Anyone can edit or delete entries on a wiki using a web browser, which often makes them biased or inaccurate. A document history is maintained. One advantage of wikis is they allow large files to be shared with others – this is much easier than emailing several people with the files.

Cambridge IGCSE ICT Study and Revision Guide © Graham Brown and David Watson, 2017

Social networking sites

These focus on building online communities of users who share similar interests and activities. They enable people to share photos, videos, hobbies, and so on. Members create public profiles allowing them to form 'relationships' with other users. Typical features of social networking sites include:

- Members can create private and public profiles using the free web space.
- It is possible to 'write' on each other's virtual walls.
- Members are given free instant messaging and video chatting.
- Members can invite other people to become 'friends' or to 'follow them'.
- Members have control over who can access private and personal data.

Search engines

These are used to find information on the internet using key words or phrases. Each web page/site found matching the search criteria is known as a 'hit'. To reduce the number of hits it is necessary to narrow down the search by including extra words, and so on. The advantages and disadvantages of using the internet and search engines to find information can be summarised:

Advantages
- Information tends to be up to date and there is almost a limitless amount of information.
- Search engines are faster ways of finding information and can be used at home rather than visiting a library, for example, when using books as the resource.
- Internet pages often have multimedia elements which can be useful; it is also easier to incorporate data into your own documents using the copy and paste facility.

Disadvantages
- The internet is not regulated; therefore, information may be biased or inaccurate.
- Inappropriate and dangerous websites are always a big risk.
- Information overload is a common problem, especially if the user is not experienced using search engines – this can make it slow to find the relevant information.
- There is an increased plagiarism risk since copy and paste is very easy to do.
- Research skills can be lost.

As mentioned above, internet material may be biased or inaccurate. However, it is possible to help safeguard yourself against this:

- Look at the final part of the URL (for example, .ac and .gov refer to education or government bodies, and so are indicators that the material may be more accurate or reliable).
- Compare information from a number of websites and, if available, check material against textbooks.
- Check if the website is endorsed by reliable/responsible bodies (sometimes you see star ratings: ★ ★ ★ ★ ☆).
- Check out any links in the website – if the links go to unreliable sites then the website itself should be avoided.
- Check when the website was last updated (if it was a long time ago the material may be well out of date).

Cambridge IGCSE ICT Study and Revision Guide © Graham Brown and David Watson, 2017

● Common errors

The difference between web browsers and ISPs is often confused or not understood:

✖ Web browsers are used to allow a user to gain access to the internet.
✔ ISPs provide the user with *access* to the internet (for a monthly fee), whereas web browsers allow the user to *view* web pages.

Sample exam questions

a Describe **four** netiquette recommendations when sending emails.

b A photographer takes many photographs as part of his work. Compare the advantages and disadvantages of using cloud storage to store the photographs rather than using portable storage devices connected to his computer.

Student's answer

a Don't use abusive language when writing emails; always check the spelling and grammar, particularly if sending out commercial emails to ensure a good impression; always remember that information in emails may become public, so be careful with the contents; don't use too many capital letters or emoticons since both can annoy recipients.

Examiner's comments

a The candidate has correctly expanded on the four recommendations indicating they have more than a cursory knowledge of the subject.

Student's answer

b Advantages:
   the photographer can access his photos anywhere from any device
   no need to carry portable storage devices around (which could be lost or stolen)
   automatic back-up of files at the end of the day
   if the user's devices malfunction, the photos could be corrupted or lost
   there is no limit to how many photos he could store.
   Disadvantages:
   there are security issues with cloud storage
   it is essential to have access to a good internet connection
   can be expensive to constantly upload and download files and to buy portable storage devices
   there is always the risk that the cloud storage company fails and there will be uncertainty about what happens to stored files.

Examiner's comments

b While the candidate has given a good balance of advantages and disadvantages they haven't fully answered the question. They were asked to make a comparison; therefore, it would be necessary to add an additional paragraph such as:

'Although buying and using cloud storage is expensive, it is still cheaper and safer than buying portable storage devices. While security risks do exist, they also still exist when using portable devices, and cloud storage gives the additional advantage of daily back-ups so that data is always up to date on all devices used.'

Examiner's tip

Questions where comparisons are to be made are best answered by giving a whole list of differences and either doing the comparison as part of the differences or by making some end statement as shown above in the examiner's comments.

Exam-style questions

1 Use the following terms to complete the five statements that follow (four of the terms will not be used).

active	*hits*	*protocols*	*data redundancy*	*netiquette*
private cloud	*encryption*	*passive*	*public cloud*	

a This term refers to the need to respect another person's views and to display a common courtesy to each other.

b A type of offline storage environment where the customer/client and provider are different companies is known as …

c Data which is stored on more than one device (for example, a server) in case of repair, maintenance or potential data loss is referred to as …

d Number of occasions where key words in a search engine match up with websites/web pages.

e Type of attack leading to a modification to a user's messages or emails or denial of services is known as … [5 marks]

2 a Explain the differences between:

public cloud

private cloud

hybrid cloud. [3 marks]

b i What is meant by the term 'netiquette'?

ii Describe **three** common rules of netiquette.

c Describe the main differences between blogs and wikis. [4 marks]

Cambridge IGCSE ICT Study and Revision Guide © Graham Brown and David Watson, 2017

File management

Key objectives

The objectives of this chapter are to revise:

- generic file types
- the use of appropriate file names

- reduction of file sizes for storage or transmission
- resizing an image
- resampling
- file compression.

Key terms

Term	Definition
Generic file type	File types that can be opened in appropriate software on most platforms.
Back-up	Copy of a file made in case the original data is corrupted or lost.
Archive	The storage of information for a long period of time. Data is likely to be compressed.
File compression	A technique for reducing the storage space occupied by a large file.

Generic file types

Common generic text file formats:

Extension	Name	Notes
.csv	**C**omma **S**eparated **V**alues	It takes data in the form of tables (that could be used with a spreadsheet or database) and saves it as text, with no formatting, separating data items with commas.
.txt	**T**e**XT**	A text file that is not formatted and can be opened in any word processor.
.rtf	**R**ich **T**ext **F**ormat	This is a text file type that saves a limited amount of formatting with the text.

Common generic image file formats:

Extension	Name	Notes
.gif	**G**raphics **I**nterchange **F**ormat	Stores still or moving images and is widely used in web pages.
.jpg or .jpeg	**J**oint **P**hotographic **E**xpert **G**roup	Stores still images and is widely used in web pages.
.pdf	**P**ortable **D**ocument **F**ormat	A document which has been converted into an image format. It allows documents to be seen as an image so they can be read on most computers. The pages look like a printed document but can contain hyperlinks, buttons, video, audio, and so on. Can be protected from editing.
.png	**P**ortable **N**etwork **G**raphics	Was created to replace Graphics Interchange Format and is now the most used lossless image compression format used on the internet.
.mp4	**M**oving **P**ictures experts group layer **4**	A multimedia container used for storing video files, still images, audio files, subtitles, and so on. It is often used to transfer video files on the internet.

Common generic audio file format:

Extension	Name	Notes
.mp3	**M**oving **P**ictures experts group layer **3**	A compressed file format with high quality yet relatively small file sizes, which makes it suitable for use on the internet.

Common generic website authoring file formats:

Extension	Name	Notes
.css	**C**ascading **S**tyle **S**heet	This is a stylesheet which is attached to one or more web pages to define the formatting of the page.
.htm or .html	**H**yper**T**ext **M**arkup **L**anguage	This is a text-based language used to create markup that a web browser will use to display information in a web page.

Common generic compressed file formats:

Extension	Name	Notes
.rar	**R**oshal **AR**chive	This is a container which can hold several files, each with different file types, in a compressed format. It is used to reduce the number of bytes needed to save a file, either to save storage space or to reduce transmission time. This was designed for the *Microsoft Windows* operating system.
.zip	Zip file	This is a container which can hold several files, each with different file types, in a compressed format. It is used to reduce the number of bytes needed to save a file, either to save storage space or to reduce transmission time.

● Saving your work

Work should always be saved using a planned folder structure using folders and sub-folders. Filenames should show a progression of work using version numbers. Use an 'old versions' folder to reduce the number of files in a working folder. Make back-ups of your work and archive files/folders to save storage space for work that is not used regularly but still needs to be kept. You can save your work in different file formats using File and Save As in many packages and using File and Export in others, particularly to export a file into portable document format (.pdf) or into a compressed file format.

● Common errors

✖ Back up and archive are the same thing.

✔ Back-ups are used to quickly recover a file when (current) data is accidentally overwritten, deleted or corrupted. It is often used to quickly recover an overwritten file or corrupted database. Archive files store version(s) of a file that needs to be used very rarely and are usually held on other media stored in a different building/location.

✖ A file saved in portable document format (.pdf) is a generic **text** file.

✔ A pdf (portable document format) file is a generic image file, as the original document has been changed into an image of the document.

Sample exam questions

a Name **three** examples of generic image file formats and for each identify the file extension. [3]

b Compare and contrast these three file formats. [6]

Student's answer

a Joint Photographic Expert Group (.jpg)
   Portable Network Graphics (.png)
   Moving Pictures experts group layer 4 (.mp4)

Examiner's comments

a The student has answered this question well, gaining all 3 marks. In a question like this, many students will submit a part of the answer and forget the name or extension.

Student's answer

b PNG and JPEG images can only support still images, whereas MP4 format supports moving images. PNG is lossless compression whereas JPEG is not.

Examiner's comments

b This response would score two of the possible 6 marks. Marks would be awarded for PNG and JPEG only supporting still images and for MP4 supporting moving images. The student has omitted the detail of MP4 being a container which can also include other elements, like still images. They are also incorrect in their statement that JPEG is not a lossless compression. The original JPEG images were saved with lossy compression but some JPEG standards now include lossless compression. There is scope for students to gain extra marks in the question by describing the differences between JPEG and PNG, for example: 'PNG was developed to replace JPEG and can contain images with a transparent background.' This answer lacks clarity because the student has not compared by identifying the similarities between each of the file formats or contrasted by identifying the differences between these formats.

> **Examiner's tip**
>
> The only way to gauge the depth required in questions like this is to look at the allocated marks and space given to write the answer; in this case it is a question worth 6 marks so students should be aiming to write between six and eight different mark points. Sometimes a number of mark points can be written into a single sentence.

● Reduce file sizes for storage and transmission ☐

File sizes need to be as small as possible as all computer systems have a limited storage capacity and it is important to minimise any delays when data is transmitted (sent) between one device and another. Often the largest files stored, or transmitted, are image files, especially video files which are a large number of still images. Still images can be reduced in size by:

- resizing, which is reducing the width and height of an image
- resampling, which is reducing the quality of an image

Resizing an image
There are two recommended methods of resizing an image. The first is to resize the image in a graphics package, for example, reducing an image 800 pixels by 600 pixels to 400 by 300 pixels. The second method of resizing is to use the cropping tool in a graphics package.

Resampling an image
Downsampling reduces the image quality and file size by reducing the number of pixels used for an image. Upsampling increases the resolution of an image by adding extra pixels.

Using file compression
Completed documents containing lots of formatting or lots of images tend to have a large file size. One way of compressing a file is to convert it into portable document format (.pdf). When you have several files it is more efficient to compress the files together in a single ZIP or RAR file.

Sample exam questions

a   Explain **two** reasons why file compression is used.   [2]

b   Explain the difference between upsampling and downsampling.   [3]

Student's answer

a *Because files are too large and it takes too long to do anything.*

Examiner's comments

a The student has answered this question poorly and would score no marks. Although they have identified large files as an issue, they have not been specific. The student should have identified the amount of storage capacity required to deal with large file sizes. They could have added that when the file is loaded or transmitted it will take considerably longer to load or transmit than a compressed file containing the same data.
It would have been better if the student had written that the transmission of smaller data files would mean fewer data packets transmitted which would lead to fewer transmission errors. This would also speed up the transmission time.

Student's answer

b *Upsampling adds more pixels to an image and downsampling removes some pixels.*

Examiner's comments

b This response would score a single mark for the student showing an understanding that pixels are added to images when upsampling or removed when downsampling. For a question worth 3 marks, much greater detail is required. For example:
  • Explain why these techniques are used: downsampling to reduce file size and upsampling to increase the resolution of an image, which would be useful if the image is to be enlarged.
  • Show an understanding that techniques such as selecting/calculating a single pixel from each block of four would reduce the file size to around a quarter of its original size.

> **Examiner's tip**
> Be specific with your answers, do not use phrases like 'It takes too long to do anything'. This should be phrased as, for example: 'It takes too long to open the web page using images with large file sizes', or 'It takes too long to transfer the data with such large file sizes'.

Exam-style questions

1 Some file types contain moving images. Identify **two** file extensions used with files containing moving images.   [2 marks]

2 Identify **three** file extensions used for generic text files.   [3 marks]

3 .rar and .zip are generic file extensions. Compare and contrast these file types.   [4 marks]

Images

Key objectives

The objectives of this chapter are to revise:

- resizing
- aspect ratio
- text wrapping
- cropping
- rotation
- reflection
- colour depth
- resolution
- brightness
- contrast.

● Key terms

Term	Definition
Resize	Change the physical size of an image.
Text wrap	Change the properties of an image to force text to flow around, over or behind it.
Cropping	Remove part of an image by cutting one or more edges from it to create an image with a different size.
Rotation	Turn an image (usually either clockwise or anticlockwise (counter-clockwise) through a specified number of degrees).
Reflection	Flip an image (usually either horizontally or vertically).
Colour depth	The number of bits used to represent each colour within a single pixel.
Aspect ratio	The ratio of the width to the height of an image.

● Editing an image

Images can be edited in many ways; they often have to be edited to fit into a pre-defined space or placeholder. How they are edited depends upon the task, but it is usual to make sure that the proportions of the image are not changed. Take care when considering the use of the image and its audience, for example, if an image is to be included on a web page then a low-resolution image may be required. However, if an image is to be included in an enlarged publication then a high-resolution image would be better to help reduce pixilation.

Resizing an image with aspect ratio maintained

Although resizing appears the easiest image editing skill, students often use the drag handles of an image without considering the loss of the aspect ratio of the image. It is better to use the 'Properties' window for the image and set the size there. This can help make sure that the aspect ratio is maintained (some software requires you to tick the 'Constrain proportions' check box). If an image size is specified on the question paper, resizing in this way makes sure that the image is exactly the right size, whereas using the drag handles is not always as accurate.

● Common errors

✖ Image is distorted when resized.

✔ The aspect ratio of an image should always be maintained when editing images, unless you have been told clearly not to do so.

Wrapping text around an image

You are able to surround (wrap) an image with text. There are a number of different types of text wrapping, which are detailed as follows:

Icon	Name	Notes
	In line with text	Image becomes an in-line graphic and is treated as a text character within the line of text. It will move if new text is inserted or deleted.
	Square	Text flows around a rectangular placeholder.
	Top and bottom	Text flows above and below the image but not alongside it.
	Tight	Text flows all around the image, but not inside if it contains white space.
	Through	Text flows all around and inside the image if it contains white space.
	Behind	Image is placed behind the text, which is ideal for watermarks in documents.
	In front	Image is placed in front of the text.

Placing an image

Where possible use the 'Position…' tab to align an image to the margins. Marks cannot be gained for the placement of an image in the practical examinations unless it has been placed precisely so that the edges of the image match one or more margin/s. Dragging images to place them is less accurate.

Adding borders to an image

Image borders can sometimes be added to show the examiner that you have placed an image precisely, especially when the image has white space around the edges.

Cropping, rotating and reflecting an image

When you crop an image you remove part of an image by cutting one or more edges from it to create an image with a different size. Rotating an image means to turn the image clockwise or counter-clockwise. Reflecting an image means to create a mirror image of it.

Cambridge IGCSE ICT Study and Revision Guide © Graham Brown and David Watson, 2017

Original

Crop

Rotate

Reflect

Adjust the colour depth of an image

The colour depth is the number of bits used to store the colour code for each pixel. There are three components (called channels) to each pixel. These are red, green and blue. The colour depth is the number of bits per channel ×3. The higher the colour depth the more colours can be displayed in the image.

Adjust the resolution of an image

The image resolution is the number of pixels per inch (or for printed documents the number of dots per inch). These are set within your graphics package. If images are low resolution (have a small number of pixels per inch) they have a smaller file size and, therefore, transfer faster than a high-resolution image which has a larger file size.

Brightness and contrast of an image

The relative brightness of an image, as well as its contrast (that is, the difference between an image's darkest and lightest areas) can both be adjusted.

Sample exam questions

a   Identify the **three** colour channels used within a JPEG image.   [1]

b   How many bits per channel are used in this file format?   [1]

c   Discuss the statement 'An image with 48-bit colour depth is more useful than the same image saved with 24-bit colour depth.'   [6]

Student's answers

a Red, Green, Blue (RGB)
b 8
c 48-bit colour depth is a better picture quality than 24-bit colour depth.

Examiner's comments

a   The student has answered this question well.

b   This is correct; the JPEG standard is 8 bits per channel (giving a 24-bit colour depth).

c   This response would score one of the possible 6 marks. This mark would be for identifying that picture quality is improved with more bits per channel. The student has omitted to identify the difference in file sizes and relative number of colours, for example: the 24-bit image would require half as much storage capacity as the 48-bit image. The 24-bit image is SVGA with over 16 million colours available, whereas the 48-bit image has 281 trillion colours available. The human eye can only determine between 10 and 12 million colours so having the extra colours may not be of huge benefit. The student could also contextualise *this – if the image was for a thumbnail for website use the file size would be more important than the image quality to decrease the download times, and so on. This answer lacks clarity because the student has not identified similarities and differences between the two values identified, nor have they expanded upon the valid point that they have made.*

Examiner's tip

This single-line answer would also be too short for a 6-mark discuss-style question where the examiner will be looking for at least six different marking points. If you make a point and add detail to it then sometimes a single sentence can be worth 2 or more marks.

Exam-style questions

1 Image A has been transformed to create images B, C and D. Identify the transformation that has been applied to image A to create each new image. [3 marks]

Image A	Image B	Image C	Image D

2 Define the term 'aspect ratio'. [1 mark]

Layout

CHAPTER 13

Key objectives

The objectives of this chapter are to revise:

- planning your document
- editing methods
- headers and footers
- automated fields.

● Key terms

Term	Definition
Header	The area at the top of a document between the top of the page and the top margin.
Footer	The area at the bottom of a document between the bottom of the page and the bottom margin.

● Planning your document

A document can be a piece of printed or electronic matter that provides information or evidence or that serves as an official record. Before starting a task, you must consider:

- What is the purpose of the document?
- Who is the target audience?
- How will I make it suitable for this audience?
- What is the appropriate medium?
- What is the appropriate package?

● Editing methods

Make sure that you know how to perform these operations on text and images:

- highlight text
- select an image
- cut and paste
- copy, paste and delete
- move, drag and drop.

Keyboard shortcuts for editing in *Microsoft Windows*:

- cut   \<Ctrl\>\<X\>
- paste   \<Ctrl\>\<V\>
- copy   \<Ctrl\>\<C\>
- redo (the last action)   \<Ctrl\>\<Y\>
- undo (the last action)   \<Ctrl\>\<Z\>

● Headers and footers

Headers and footers are the areas at the top and bottom of every page in a document and are often used to display information like the author's name, the date of creation and the name of the document. Because headers and footers are often common to all pages, data only has to be entered once. This saves time and reduces the chance of data entry errors.

Cambridge IGCSE ICT Study and Revision Guide © Graham Brown and David Watson, 2017

It is illegal to photocopy this page

In some packages it is possible to set different headers and footers for different pages or sections of a document, for example you can choose not to display a header or footer on the first page. This is useful as, when books or booklets are being produced, facing pages may contain different information, using different settings for the left and right pages.

Automated fields

Automated fields can be placed in many types of document and are most commonly used to place items in the header or footer. This includes items like page numbering, an automated filename and file path, today's date, and so on. Other automated fields can be placed elsewhere in documents.

Study the headers and footers used in this book and the Cambridge IGCSE ICT Coursebook. Do you think these contain automated fields?

● Common errors

✖ Contents are placed in a header or footer but not aligned to the page margins.
✔ Make sure you align all headers and footers to the page margins, especially when working within a word processor.

Aligning headers and footers

For any word-processed document that you produce, it is essential that the margins on the header and footer match the margins of the page. If you are using *Microsoft Word*, change the positioning of the header and footer to align with the page margins using tab stops on the ruler (see page 215 in the Cambridge IGCSE ICT Coursebook for details on this).

Sample exam question

A report of 68 pages has been created for a customer. The report contains headers and footers. Explain, using examples, why headers and footers are used. [4]

Student's answer

Headers and footers are used to insert page elements that need to be present in all pages, like the page number.

Examiner's comments

This answer is worth two of the 4 available marks. It starts well, and the identification that page elements are placed on all pages would gain credit, but the student could have included why it is an advantage to use this method rather than typing the elements on every page (less time required to enter/edit and less chance of errors). This would have turned the initial answer from a single mark into three. The page number on each page would also gain a second mark, but again there is scope for this student to identify other elements that may have been placed in the header or footer, like an automated filename and file path, the title of the report or the author's name.

Sample exam question

List **two** items that would be appropriate to place in the header or footer of a report to show the storage capacities of Solid State Drives (SSD).   [2]

Student's answer

Page number

The author's favourite football team

The author's name

The file name and path of the document.

Examiner's comments

This would only gain one of the 2 available marks. The page number would gain a mark, the second answer is clearly inappropriate for this task so would gain no mark. As this is a list question and has asked for two answers, all subsequent answers (even though they are correct) will not be marked.

Exam-style questions

1 Identify **four** items of information that it would be appropriate to place in the header or footer of a textbook. Do not include objects that would be placed using automated fields.   [4 marks]

2 Identify **four** items of information that it would be appropriate to place in the header or footer of a textbook using automated fields.   [4 marks]

Key objectives

The objectives of this chapter are to revise:

- corporate house styles
- font styles and sizes
- create and edit styles in a word-processed document
- using format painter
- using lists.

● Key terms

Term	Definition	
Body text	The basic style of text within a document, usually used for all of the paragraphs.	
Ascender	The part of a lowercase letter (b, d, f, h, k, l or t) that extends above the body of the letters.	text^{ascender}
Descender	The part of a lowercase letter (g, j, p, q or y) that falls below the baseline of the letters.	your_{descender}
Serif	A font style where the ends of characters contain small strokes called serifs, for example, Times New Roman.	
Sans serif	A font style where the ends of characters do not contain small strokes called serifs, for example, Arial.	

● Corporate house style

This is branding that makes a company recognisable. This can be used on something belonging to or sent from that company. House style often includes a logo, colour schemes, font styles and other features, and will be consistently applied to anything produced by the company. House style can be used on letter heads, websites, vehicles, posters, presentations, television advertising and other media. As well as ensuring a uniform and professional look across a company's documents and media, a house style also helps give a company an identity, and can help with brand recognition. If styles are specified in the examination you must apply them using the pre-defined styles, especially in the document production, presentation authoring and website authoring questions.

Font styles and sizes

When you create a new style, you will be required to set font faces and sizes. Different packages use different named fonts, so (with the exception of website authoring) generic names will be used rather than specific font names. The generic names fall into two main categories: serif and sans serif (there are others but they are beyond the scope of IGCSE).

You will not find serif and sans serif as named fonts in your applications package, but Times New Roman is an example of a serif font, while Arial is an example of a sans serif font (as it does not have serifs on the letters).

● Common errors

✖ Students write a note on the exam paper saying 'My computer does not have a font called serif so I used …'
✔ Use **Times New Roman** as the serif font if you are using *Microsoft Office*.
✖ Students write a note on the exam paper saying 'My computer does not have a font called sans serif so I used …'
✔ Use **Arial** as the sans serif font if you are using *Microsoft Office*.

Font sizes are measured in points; there are 72 points to an inch (just over 2.5 centimetres). If the question does not specify a point size, make the text readable for the audience specified, for example: a minimum of 10 points high for body text, 12 points high for older readers and at least 20 points for young children learning to read.

The size of a font is measured from the top of the letter with the tallest ascender (often the letter 'h'), to the bottom of the one with the longest descender (often the letter 'f', though note that the typeface chosen for this book does not have a descender on the 'f'! Many do, however: *f̵ f, f, f, f,).*

● Create and edit styles in a word-processed document

When using *Microsoft Word*, styles are saved in a document's template file. Open the document and format one area of text within the document to match the required styles. Highlight this formatted area of text and use it to create a new style (see page 222 in the Cambridge IGCSE ICT Coursebook for details) with its own style name. Make sure that the style name matches that shown in the question paper, including the case (capitals and lower case letters) and any special characters (like the hyphen - or underscore _). Now highlight any other area/s where this text should be applied and click on the style you have defined, in the Styles section of the Home tab. Use this tab to edit the styles defined for this document. Please note, *Microsoft Word* calls this Modify Styles rather than edit, as in the syllabus.

● Common errors

✖ When asked to show how styles have been defined, students screen shot only the first part of this process, that is, applying the individual style elements to the text.
✔ When asked to show how styles have been defined, show the examiner the whole of the Modify Style window for the specified style. Check that all of the style elements from the question paper can be seen in this window, including the spacing before and after the paragraph. These can often be seen in the text listing at the bottom of the modify window.

Using format painter

The format painter tool ✔ which can be found in the Home tab in most *Microsoft Office* packages is ideal for copying formatting from one part of a document to another. This works in packages like the spreadsheet *Excel,* which do not allow you to use defined styles in the same way as *Microsoft Word.*

Using lists

There are two types of list: numbered lists (which can include lettering and roman numerals, and so on) and bulleted lists. Make sure that you can change between the two types in both *Microsoft Word* and *Microsoft Excel.* In the word processor make sure that you are confident using tab stops on the ruler (see page 215 in the Cambridge IGCSE ICT Coursebook) so that you can indent the bullet points (or numbers) by a particular distance from the page or column margin.

Lists can have many levels, like this (note that when one list is placed inside another, this is known as a nested list):

- This is a first-level list
- This is a first-level list
  ○ This is a second-level list
  ○ This is a second-level list
    ❖ This is a third-level list
    ❖ This is a third-level list
  ○ This is a second-level list
- This is a first-level list
- This is a first-level list

Sample exam question

Describe the lists used in this section of this document. [6]

> **Topics covered so far in chapter 14**
>
> While studying chapter 14, I have learnt how to:
> 1 create new styles for:
>   a) headers
>   b) footers
>   c) body text
>   d) headings
>   e) subheadings
> 2 edit styles after they have been defined
> 3 set font styles and sizes
> 4 emphasise text
> 5 use format painter
> 6 use lists.

Student's answer

There are two numbered lists, one inside another and no bulleted lists.

Cambridge IGCSE ICT Study and Revision Guide © Graham Brown and David Watson, 2017

Examiner's comments

The student has correctly identified that there are two numbered lists and that they are nested. These elements would each gain 1 mark. The student has not mentioned that there are two different levels, the level 1 list being numeric. The level 2 list (while still technically a numbered list) being in lower-case alphabetical order. The student could have identified the level 1 list having bullet points indented 3 cm from the margin and the level 2 list being indented a further 1 cm from the level 1 list (4 cm from the margin). Another element omitted by the student is that both list styles have the same font face and font size.

> **Examiner's tip**
> The question asks the student to describe the lists so it is acceptable and even desirable to extend the answer from the list styles set for each level to include the final statement of elements common to both lists. 'Describe' questions often lend themselves to answers that include similarities (which students often omit) as well as differences, especially where there is more than one element being described.

Exam-style questions

1 Describe the differences between a serif and a sans serif font.   [2 marks]

2 Define the term 'corporate house style'.   [1 mark]

3 Give **four** advantages of using a corporate house style.   [4 marks]

Proofing

Key objectives

The objectives of this chapter are to revise:

- spell check
- grammar check
- proofing techniques
- ensuring the accuracy of data entry.

● Key terms

Term	Definition
Spell check	A process where the software identifies words which are not held within its dictionary.
Grammar check	A process where the software identifies language which does not follow the accepted or expected rules.
Widow	A last line of a paragraph that appears at the top of a page/column, with the rest of the paragraph on the previous page/column.
Orphan	The first line of a paragraph that appears at the bottom of the page/column, with the rest of the paragraph on the next page/column.

Spell check

This is usually found in word-processing software. Spell check compares each word in a document against those words held in its dictionary. If a word in the document does not match the dictionary it is flagged as a possible error using a red wavy underline like this: speeling

Be aware that words that are spelled correctly but which are not included in the dictionary your spell check is using will still be flagged as possible errors. Examples of this are names, or words from a different language.

Word-processing software will often give you a list of alternative spellings to unknown words. These can be found by clicking the right mouse button on the word itself.

Sample exam questions

a A student word processes the sentence: 'We visited the Tawara Beach Hotel.' The text is spell checked.

  Explain why the word Tawara is flagged as an error. [3]

b Write down an example of text that does not contain a spelling error, but may be flagged as a spelling error by the word processor. [1]

c Explain why your answer to part b is flagged as an error. [2]

Student's answer

a There is no such word as 'Tawara' so the spell check program cannot find it. It could be added to the dictionary by the user.

Examiner's comments

a The student has not identified that the word 'Tawara' does not exist *within the dictionary* because it is the name of a hotel, so the first sentence does not gain any marks. The second sentence does mention the dictionary but there is no link between the two parts of the answer. This sentence is worth a mark as the student has recognised that the word is spelled correctly and should be added to the dictionary. It would have been a stronger answer if they had gone on to suggest that by adding the word 'Tawara' to their dictionary this would not be flagged as an error if this word was used again.

Student's answer

b We did not not arrive at the hotel on time.

Examiner's comments

b This is a correct answer.

Student's answer

c The repeated word would be shown as a spelling error even though it is a error in grammar.

Examiner's comments

c This answer would gain the marks as it clearly identifies the repeated word as the error and expands upon the answer to identify that it is a grammatical error rather than a spelling error.

Grammar check

This is usually found in word-processing software. A grammar check reviews the entered text to see if it follows the accepted or expected rules for the grammar of the language used. A simple example is that each sentence starts with a capital letter. Possible errors in grammar are shown using a blue wavy underline like this: need to make sure.

During practical examinations, do not attempt to correct any grammar errors unless they are in text that you have typed, for example; the answer to a theory question.

Validation and verification

See Chapter 7 for details on these areas.

Proofing techniques

The term 'proofing' in printing means to make sure that the work is accurate. Carefully check all spelling, punctuation, grammar and page layout. Page layout should include:

- Applying styles
- Margin settings
- Images placed with correct dimensions and no distortion
- Text wrap around images and other objects
- Objects fitting within the boundaries of a page/column/slide and not overlapping
- No lists or tables split over two columns/pages/slides
- No blank pages or slides
- No widows or orphans.

Cambridge IGCSE ICT Study and Revision Guide © Graham Brown and David Watson, 2017

Checking each of these carefully and correcting where necessary (often using page or column breaks) should help you score higher marks on the practical papers. Consistent layout and consistent styles are very important.

Ensuring the accuracy of data entry
It is important to be accurate when entering data. Inaccurate data entry is one of the most significant reasons that students lose marks in their practical examinations. Check all data entry carefully!

● Common errors

✖ Placing upper or lower case letters in the wrong place.
✔ Check that all sentences start with a capital letter and do not have capitals in the middle of a sentence. It is fine to have the word I, or names starting with capitals, in the middle of a sentence.

✖ Numbers are transposed (they change places) as they are entered, for example: the year two thousand and two entered as 2020 rather than 2002.
✔ Use visual verification to check that every character has been entered as it is in the original. Check the data entry, then check it again.

✖ Errorsin spacing   in the sentence, either by missing spaces or adding too many.
✔ Use visual verification to check that every character has been entered as it is in the original. Check that spacing is consistent throughout the document.

Examiner's tips
- If a question asks you to spell check and proof read your document, apply all of the techniques listed in this chapter to make sure that all spelling, spacing and style errors have been removed.
- Always check the accuracy of all data entry.
- Remember: **Check all data entry for errors, correct them, then check it again.**

Exam-style questions

1 This text was entered into a word processor:

'The new airport will be constructed on marshhland on the outskirts of Tawara.'

The spell check suggests there are two errors. Identify each suggested error and explain why it may or may not be an error.   [4 marks]

2 This text was entered into a word processor:

'Mrs jones works as an examiner. He marks your examination papers.'

Identify any errors in this text   [2 marks]

Cambridge IGCSE ICT Study and Revision Guide © Graham Brown and David Watson, 2017

Graphs and charts

Key objectives

The objectives of this chapter are to revise:

- chart types
- creating a chart
- labelling a chart
- secondary axes.

● Key terms

Term	Definition
Contiguous data	Data that is placed together and can be selected in a single range.
Non-contiguous data	Data that is not placed together (often in a spreadsheet) and cannot be selected using a single range.
X-axis	The horizontal axis (for a system of co-ordinates).
Y-axis	The vertical axis (for a system of co-ordinates).
Category axis	A name given to the chart axis in *Microsoft Office* that represents the category for each data point. It displays text values.
Value axis	A name given to the chart axis in *Microsoft Office* that displays numerical values.
Legend	A box that identifies the patterns or colours that show different data series in a chart.

● Chart types

You may be asked to select an appropriate chart type to answer a question. For the IGCSE exam there are three types to choose from: a pie chart, a bar chart or a line graph. When considering what chart to use, you must first consider what the graph is supposed to show.

Use a:

- **pie chart** to compare parts of a whole, for example, the percentage of boys and girls in a class
- **bar chart** to show the difference between things, for example, the number of times Ahmed, Ben, Carla and Dee went shopping in a week
- **line graph** to plot trends between two variables, for example, plotting the distance a person travelled in 10 minutes recorded in 1-minute intervals.

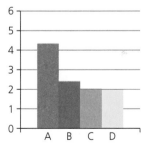
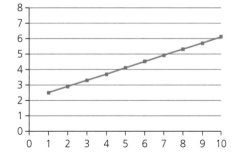

Sample exam questions

a Identify the most appropriate graph or chart to display:

  i a comparison between distance travelled and time taken for a teacher to drive home

  ii the number of oranges eaten this year by eight students

  iii the percentages of people in a class with different hair colours

  iv a comparison between the interest rate (shown as a percentage) offered by three banks.

b The following data will be used to create a new graph or chart.

Time in seconds	0	1	2	3	4	5	6	7	8
Distance travelled in metres	0	2	5	8	12	16	16	12	6

  i State the type of graph or chart that will be most appropriate.

  ii Explain why this is the most appropriate type.   [6]

Student's answers

a i A line graph.
  ii A bar chart.
  iii A pie chart.
  iv A pie chart.
b i A line graph.
  ii Because a distance-time graph plots the trends between two variables.

Examiner's comments

a i This is a correct answer.
  ii This is a correct answer.
  iii This is a correct answer.
  iv This is not the correct answer. The student has not read the question carefully. Because this question mentions the word 'percentage', which would normally indicate a pie chart is suitable, that is the answer that has been given. This question does not ask for parts of a whole but is comparing different rates from different banks. The correct answer to this question would have been a bar chart.
b i This is a correct answer.
  ii This is an excellent answer identifying that this is a comparison between distance travelled and time, so, therefore, the line graph plots the trends between these two variables.

Creating a chart

Create a graph or chart by highlighting the data to be used for the graph or chart. If the data is non-contiguous then hold down the <Ctrl> key as you select the two (or more) ranges of data. Select the chart type, using the notes above on appropriate chart types to help you. Make sure that you fully label the chart.

Cambridge IGCSE ICT Study and Revision Guide © Graham Brown and David Watson, 2017

Labelling a chart

All charts must be fully labelled. Make sure that all of the text in all titles, labels and in the legend, is fully visible. It is usual to label a pie chart with segment labels *or* a legend, but not both.

Sample exam question

A trainee has created the following bar chart to show the director of a software company how many members of staff work in each job type within a branch:

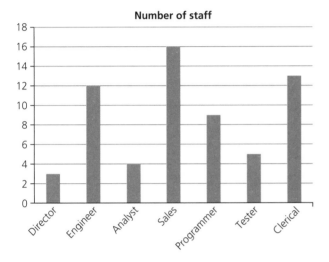

Discuss the suitability of this chart for this task. [6]

Student's answer

This chart contains a chart title and both category and value axis labels but does not tell you what the chart shows. A category axis title and value axis title are both needed, as well as more detail in the chart title, so that the user can understand the data without referring elsewhere for its meaning.

Examiner's comments

This is the start of a very good answer worth four of the 6 marks. It identifies the title and axis labels as being present, then focuses on the omissions from the chart. To answer this 'discuss' question, a number of positive and negative points should be present. For example, that the title, category and value axis labels are not only present but fully visible, clear, easy to read and in appropriate font sizes for the audience. The chart type is also appropriate for the data being presented. One mark could also have been attained for a reasoned conclusion, gained by balancing the positive and negative points to suggest that the chart is suitable or unsuitable for its purpose, depending upon the strength of arguments for each side made by the student.

Secondary axes

Secondary axes are added to a line graph (or combined line and bar chart) when two data sets are plotted on the same graph with very different sets of values. The chart shown here (created in Task 16f on pages 246–48 of the Cambridge IGCSE ICT Coursebook) is an ideal example of this:

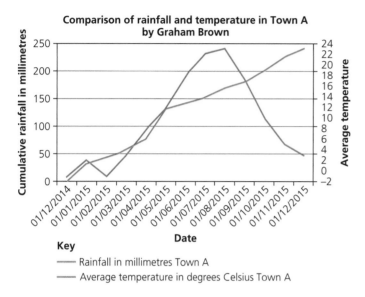

Key
— Rainfall in millimetres Town A
— Average temperature in degrees Celsius Town A

The two sets of data show rainfall data between 0 and almost 250 millimetres and temperatures between –1 and 23 degrees Celsius. As these are very different sets of data, two axes are required, one for the rainfall and one for the temperature. In this example, the axes have also been edited to make them easier to read and compare.

If you are required to create a comparative line graph, check to see if the two data sets are the same type of data; if not, add a secondary axis to the graph.

Sample exam questions

Explain why three axes will be needed when creating a chart from this data: [4]

2016 temperature and snowfall data for Keystone, Colorado	January	February	March	April	May	June	July	August	September	October	November	December
Average minimum temperature °C	–18	–16	–11	–7	–3	1	4	3	–1	–6	–11	–16
Monthly snow (cm)	38	38	48	38	22	3	0	0	4	17	38	46

Student's answer

The two sets of data are different.

Cambridge IGCSE ICT Study and Revision Guide © Graham Brown and David Watson, 2017

Examiner's comments

This answer is too vague. The student should mention why the data sets that would be plotted against the category axis are very different; one is a temperature in degrees Celsius and the other is the number of centimetres of snow that had fallen in the town of Keystone. To obtain more marks the student should also identify that the temperature axis and snowfall axis could be scaled. An example of this could be: 'The minimum temperature axis should range from +5 to −20 in intervals of 5 degrees, and the snowfall should range from 0 to 50 in intervals of 10 centimetres.'

● Common errors

✖ Only partially labelling graphs or charts.
✔ Fully label all graphs and charts, taking into account the audience. Make sure the chart can be understood if presented to the audience without any explanation of supporting data/materials.

Exam-style question

1 *Bar chart   Pie chart   Line graph   None of these*

From the choices listed above, select the most appropriate way of graphically representing the following:

   a The percentage of a class of students who are boys and the percentage who are girls.

   b The distance travelled by a car over periods of time.

   c The height plotted against the weight for each student in a school.

   d The height of a student when the readings are taken every week for a year.   [4 marks]

Document production

Key objectives

The objectives of this chapter are to revise:

- page size
- page orientation
- page and gutter margins
- widows and orphans
- page, section and column breaks
- text alignment
- line spacing
- tabulation settings
- tables and bulleted lists
- mail-merged documents.

● Key terms

Term	Definition
Gutter	The part of a document, usually white space outside the page margin, where the document will be bound together.
Widow	The last line of text of a paragraph that appears at the top of a page, with the rest of the paragraph on the previous page.
Orphan	The first line of text of a paragraph that appears at the bottom of the page, with the rest of the paragraph appearing on the next page.
Indented paragraph	The first line of a paragraph is indented from a margin and all other lines are aligned to the margin.
Hanging paragraph	The first line of a paragraph is aligned to a margin and all other lines are indented (left hanging from the first line).

Page size

Source files for document production questions are likely to be set to a different page size to that required for the final document, especially if they are in rich text format (.rtf). Use the Layout tab, and find the Page Setup section to change the paper size. The most commonly used page size is A4.

Page orientation

There are two types of page orientation, portrait and landscape. These are also selected from the Page Setup section in the Layout tab.

Page and gutter margins

The Page Setup section in the Layout tab also contains an area where settings for the margin (the border surrounding a page) can be changed. In any examination with document production questions this skill will be required. Take great care to set the margins as specified. The gutter size and position can also be changed here. If a gutter is required, you will need to work out where the gutter will need to be on the page. For a traditional book (or booklet) it is often on the left of the first page, but if the document is to be bound at the top of the page (for example, like some calendars) then select the top.

Cambridge IGCSE ICT Study and Revision Guide © Graham Brown and David Watson, 2017

● Common errors

✖ Setting the margin and/or gutter settings in the wrong units, for example, in inches when centimetres are required.

✔ Check the units carefully, the computer that you are using may have its software set to work in inches rather than centimetres. You will need to set the margin/gutter settings in centimetres by typing the units in the dropdown box as well as the size.

✖ Setting the page margins correctly but not adjusting the margins in the header and footer to match.

✔ Edit the margin settings in the header and footer to match the page margins.

Widows and orphans

Widows and orphans can occur at the top and bottom of a column as well as at the start and end of a page. *Microsoft Word* will attempt to remove widows and orphans for you (if this has been set up when it was installed) but it will not find all the problems, like keeping headings and the content that follows it together. When you have finished your document, carefully check for widows and orphans and insert page, column or section breaks (whichever is appropriate for the task) to remove them.

● Common errors

✖ Removing widows and orphans by continually pressing the <Enter> or <Return> key.

✔ Use either a page, column or section break to remove widows and orphans.

✖ Placing a page or column break after every paragraph to make sure there are no widows or orphans.

✔ When removing widows or orphans, leave at least two lines of paragraph text at the top and bottom of each page/column. It is better to split paragraphs as seen in example A, rather than as seen in example B:

A

B

Cambridge IGCSE ICT Study and Revision Guide © Graham Brown and David Watson, 2017

● Page, section and column breaks

A **page break** forces the text on to the start of a new page, leaving white space at the end of the previous page.

A **column break** forces the text into the top of the next available column, which may be on the same page or may be on the next page.

A **section break** can be used to split areas of a document with different layouts; it can force a page break (if selected) or be continuous, which allows different layouts on the same page (for example, a title across the whole page width when the text is placed in three columns).

Text alignment

Text can be aligned in four basic ways:

- **Left aligned** – it is aligned with a straight left margin and a ragged right margin.
- **Centre aligned** – it is aligned to the centre of the page and has ragged left and right margins.
- **Right aligned** – it is aligned with a straight right margin and a ragged left margin.
- **Fully justified** – it is aligned with straight left and right margins.

Use these icons in the Paragraph section of the Home tab after highlighting the text:

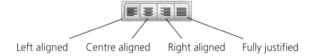

Left aligned   Centre aligned   Right aligned   Fully justified

Line spacing

Line spacing is usually set as part of a pre-defined style. The most commonly used layouts in the practical examinations are single line spacing, 1.5 line spacing and double line spacing. Use the ↕☰ ▾ icon in the Paragraph section of the Home tab.

● Common errors

✖ Not setting consistent line spacing throughout the document.
✔ Set the line spacing in your defined styles and apply these styles to all the text (of that type). There may be different settings for body style, headings, lists and tables.

Tabulation settings

Tabulation, margins and column widths can all be set using the ruler. These settings affect how each paragraph appears on the page.

Cambridge IGCSE ICT Study and Revision Guide © Graham Brown and David Watson, 2017

Sample exam question

Here are some images showing the ruler used in a word-processing document:

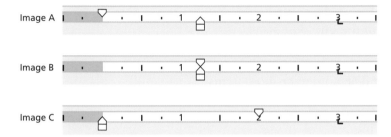

For each image, name and describe the type of paragraph that these tabulation settings produce. [9]

Student's answers

a Image A is a hanging paragraph.
b Image B is a normal paragraph.
c Image C is an indented paragraph.

Examiner's comments

All three answers have the correct names, each of these would gain this student a mark and would score three of the 9 marks. The question asks the student to name and describe; therefore, 2 marks have been lost on each part as there is no attempt to describe each type of paragraph. Adding descriptions such as these would have helped this student gain full marks:

a A hanging paragraph has the first line of each paragraph aligned to the left of the rest of the paragraph. The rest of the paragraph would sit to the right of the left margin. Only the first line of each paragraph will touch the left margin.
b Each paragraph has the first line aligned with the rest of the paragraph; in this case both are indented 1.25 units from the left margin.
c The first line of each paragraph is indented 2 units to the right of the other lines in each paragraph.

Examiner's tip
Note how in parts b and c of the examiner's comments the sizes have been taken from the images. As the images give no units of measurement, like centimetres or inches, it is acceptable to refer to them as units.

Tables and bulleted lists

A table can be edited in a number of ways. Rows and columns can be inserted or deleted. Individual cells can be merged together to create larger single cells either within one row or column, or across multiple rows or columns.

You can align data within individual cells horizontally and vertically. Horizontally you can align data left, right, centre or fully justified, while vertically you can align data to the top, centre or bottom of the cell. Other formatting techniques include choosing whether to show or hide gridlines, wrap text within a cell and add a shaded or coloured background to a cell.

Make sure that no tables or bulleted lists are split over two columns or pages. Use a column or page break to make them fit the column or page.

If they are so large that they will not fit, you are likely to have an error. Possible causes of such errors are:

- that the page size is smaller than specified in the question paper
- that the page orientation is not as specified in the question paper
- that the font size is larger than specified in the question paper
- that the line spacing is larger than specified in the question paper
- that the spacing before and after the style set for the list or table is larger than specified in the question paper
- in a numbered or bulleted list, you have not deleted one or more items specified on the question paper
- if a table is the result of a database search, then there may be an error in the criteria used in the query
- in a table, you have not deleted the rows or columns specified in the question paper
- in a table, use the ruler to adjust the column widths (unless they are specified in the question paper) to reduce the number of rows used and allow for more efficient use of the space within the table.

Examiner's tips

- If you have checked and corrected all the possible causes listed above and the table or bulleted list still does not fit within a single column or page, remembering to make sure the text is still legible, change the font face used in your style definition to a narrower font. This will allow more characters on each line, which may help.

- In a table, do not allow the text within the table to sit outside the column or page margins.

Mail-merged documents

A mail-merged document is produced by merging data from a source file with a master document to produce personalised documents, often letters. It is usually a fully automated process. Using mail merge can reduce the number of input errors, as well as significantly decreasing the time it takes to produce a large number of personalised documents.

The process for creating a mail-merged letter is to:

- open or create a master document
- add any special fields (like automated date fields) into the master document.
- create a data source file
- attach the source file to the master document
- check the source file is attached (using the Mail Merge Recipients window)
- add merge fields to the master document
- run the mail merge (selecting some or all of the data from the source file)
- check that the merged documents are those required
- check that the pagination of the merged documents is correct (correcting using page breaks if not)
- print the merged documents.

Examiner's tip

Toggle the merge codes by clicking the right mouse button on the fields and selecting from the menu before showing this in your evidence document.

Cambridge IGCSE ICT Study and Revision Guide © Graham Brown and David Watson, 2017

Sample exam question

Explain why a company would use a mail-merged document to produce 500 personalised letters.   [4]

Student's answer

It saves retyping or editing lots of documents. It takes lots of time to change 500 letters and costs lots of money to pay staff. It reduces errors as documents only have to be checked once.

Examiner's comments

This is an excellent answer gaining all 4 marks. The student has realised the need to retype or edit and has added two mark points from that: the time taken to change the letters and the potential reduction in errors. They have also gone on to enhance the first of these mark points by identifying that the time taken by staff would have a financial implication for the business.

> **Examiner's tip**
> When you add a new mark point to your answer, try to add more detail to (expand upon) this to gain a second mark.

Exam-style questions

1 Explain what is meant by the term 'margin' within a document.   [2 marks]

2 Explain what is meant by the term 'fully justified text' within a document.   [2 marks]

3 Describe what is meant by a 'hanging paragraph'. [2 marks]

4 Tuition fees will be increasing at the University of Tawara. The amount that they will increase depends upon the course being studied. Personalised letters will be sent to all 5450 students telling them of the increase.

   Explain why a mail-merged letter would be used for this task.   [4 marks]

Cambridge IGCSE ICT Study and Revision Guide © Graham Brown and David Watson, 2017

Data manipulation

CHAPTER **18**

Key objectives

The objectives of this chapter are to revise:

- database structures
- flat-file and relational databases
- data types

- form design
- searching for subsets of data
- extracting summary data
- producing reports
- sorting data.

● Key terms

Term	Definition
Field	A place used to hold a single data item in a database.
Record	A collection of fields containing information about one data subject (usually a person) in a database.
File	A logically organised collection of records, usually where all the records are organised so that they can be stored together in a database.
Table	A two-dimensional grid of data organised by rows and columns within a database. Each row of the table contains a record. Each column in the table represents a field and each cell in that column has the same (pre-defined) data type.
Flat-file database	A database structure using a simple two-dimensional table.
Relational database	A database structure where data items are linked together using relational tables. It maintains a set of separate, related files (tables), but combines data elements from the files for queries and reports when required.
Primary key field	A single field within a relational database table that contains unique data (no two records within this field can contain the same data). A primary key field cannot contain a blank record.
Foreign key field	A field in one database table that provides a link/creates a relationship to a primary key field in another database table.
Query	A request for information from a database.
Report (generic)	A document that provides information.
Report (*Microsoft Access*)	The formatted and organised presentation of data from a database.
Data capture form	A form used for collecting data for input to a system, which can be hard copy or screen-based.
Data entry form	A screen-based form used to input data into a system.

Database structures

A database is a program used to store data in a structured way. A database includes both the data itself, and the links between the data items.

All databases store data using fields, records and files.

Fields Each is a single item of data and has a fieldname, which is used to identify it within the database. Each field contains one type of data, for example, numbers, text, or a date. All field names should be short, meaningful and contain no spaces.

Records Each record is a collection of fields, for example, all the information about one person or one item. These may contain different data types.

Files Each file is an organised collection of records stored together. A file can have one or more tables within it.

It is illegal to photocopy this page

Cambridge IGCSE ICT Study and Revision Guide © Graham Brown and David Watson, 2017

Flat-file database
A flat-file database has a simple structure where data is held in a two-dimensional table and is organised by rows and columns. This is stored in a single file.

A flat-file database is suitable for use with one type of data (for example, data about customers, cars or CDs) that does not contain large quantities of duplicated data.

Relational database
A relational database stores the data in more than one linked table, stored in a single file. It is designed to reduce duplicated data. Each table has a key field. Most tables have a primary key field, which holds unique data (no two records are the same in this field) and is the field used to identify that record. Some tables will have one or more foreign key fields. A foreign key in one table will link to a primary key in another table. This makes relational databases more efficient when storing data, as an item of data is stored only once rather than many times. Storing the data only once reduces the time taken to add or edit data (and, therefore, the cost of employing workers) and reduces the chance of errors. It also means less storage capacity will be required, so it can reduce the initial hardware costs, especially for very large databases.

A relational database is suitable for use with more than one type of data that are related (for example, cars sold and customers), or with data that contains large quantities of duplicated data.

● Common errors

✖ Relational databases can give search results more quickly than flat-file databases.

✔ The relative speed of the same search on the same data using a flat-file database and a relational database is dependent on the structures of the data tables in the relational database and the quantity of data being searched.

Data types
There are three main data types. These are:

Alphanumeric This is used to store text and numbers not used for calculations. In *Microsoft Access* this is called a 'text' field, or in later versions either 'short text' or 'long text'.

Numeric This is used to store numbers. In *Microsoft Access* this is usually called a 'number' field and has several sub-types, such as:

- Integer – which stores whole numbers. In *Microsoft Access* it is better to use the 'long integer' sub-type.
- Decimal – which stores decimal numbers.
- Currency – which displays local currency formatting. In *Microsoft Access* this is called a currency data type, although it is technically a sub-type.
- Date and Time – in *Microsoft Access* this displays the date in a recognised date format but stores the date and/or time as a number.

Boolean This is used to store data as 0 or −1 to represent Yes/No, True/False. In *Microsoft Access* this is called a 'Yes/No' field.

Apart from these three main data types, *Microsoft Access* also includes an 'autonumber' field. This is an automatically generated unique data field, which can be used to index and organise data.

Sample exam question

Anna is the principal of a college. She has employed a systems analyst to create a new database system to store records of her A-level students.

Examples of the details of some students which will be stored are:

- Nadia Nowak, C3058, Female, 174, Not University
- Alfons Lisowski, C3072, Male, 177, University
- Nicola Menossi, F3888, Female, 173, Not University
- Giovanni Agnelli, D3012, Male, 192, University

Copy and complete the following data dictionary by entering the field names and most appropriate data type for each field. For any numeric field, specify the sub-type. [5]

Field name	Data type
Forename	
	Boolean
Height	

Student's answer

Field name	Data type
Forename	Text
Second name	Alphanumeric
Student_ID	Alphanumeric
Gender	Boolean
Height	Numeric – integer
Post_18	Boolean

Examiner's comments

The data type for the Forename field should have been identified as Alphanumeric which is the correct name for this data type; however, as Text is the field type used in some software, examiners would be likely to credit the student with this mark. The field name that should have been Surname, Second_Name or Family_Name contains a space so would be unlikely to gain a mark. The data type for this field, though, is correct. The student_ID and its data type are both correct answers. The field name Gender is an appropriate field name for this Boolean data. The data type for Height is an excellent answer indicating both the data type and sub-type. For the last row, field names such as Post_18 or After_College are fine, and the student has recognised that the data in the field has two possible conditions so it is Boolean.

Examiner's tips
- Take great care to follow the naming conventions for field names used in the question; if underscores are used instead of spaces, continue this convention in your field names.
- Remember to keep all field names short, meaningful and containing no spaces. Examine the question carefully before attempting to answer it.

Form design

Forms can include data-capture forms, which are often created on paper to collect the data to add to a database, or online data-entry forms. All these forms should have the following features:

- A title
- Instructions on completing the form
- Appropriate font styles and sizes for the target audience
- Clear easy-to-read questions (closed questions where possible)
- Boxes (or other indication of space) for the answers
- Appropriate sizes for the answer boxes (not all the same size)
- Similar fields grouped into blocks/categories (for example, all address fields together)
- No crowding of fields (all should have white space between)
- The form fills the page
- No large areas of white space
- Only relevant data collected.

Online data-entry forms should also have navigation buttons; to submit/ save the data (and move to the next record), clear the form, close the form, minimise the form, move to the first record, previous record, quit, and so on. Where online forms are being designed the use of radio buttons or dropdown menus should be used where possible.

Searching for subsets of data

Access queries are used to search for data. They can be simple queries using single criterion or more complex queries using multiple criteria. Queries can contain equalities using = and LIKE, or inequalities using >, >=, <, =<, and <>. The three Boolean statements AND, OR and NOT can also be included in your queries. The * key will allow you to perform wildcard searches.

Sample exam question

A database contains the following data about meal costs at venues in England:

Meals				
Venue	*Town*	*County*	*Meal_Cost*	*Guests*
Flying Fox	ASHFORD	KENT	12.95	3
Freddie's	ASHFORDLY	YORKSHIRE	16.30	5
Korma Kurry	BRADFORD	YORKSHIRE	24.10	2
Yellow Goose	BRENTFORD	MIDDLESEX	23.00	2
Cricketer's Arms	FORDHAM	ESSEX	12.50	5
Patel's Pantry	SHEFFIELD	YORKSHIRE	9.65	16
White Swan	SKIPTON	YORKSHIRE	14.20	4

List the results which would be output when the following search criteria are used on the Town field:

a   *FORD

b   FORD*

c   *FORD*   [3]

Student's answers

a ASHFORD, BRADFORD
b FORDHAM
c ASHFORD, ASHFORDLY, BRADFORD, BRENTFORD, FORDHAM

Examiner's comments

a The student has found the first two towns ending with the word FORD but has omitted the town of BRENTFORD.
b This is correct, the student has found the only town starting with FORD.
c This is correct, the student has found all the towns containing the word FORD.

> **Examiner's tip**
>
> This is a good example of a typical IGCSE answer where the student understands the question yet has, in part a missed out one of the answers. A good examination technique is to read the question, answer it, read the same question again, then check that the answer is correct. This technique can make a significant difference to your performance in the final examinations.

● Common errors

✖ The default setting in the query wizard (in some versions of *Access*) is to the last query or table that you used. Where two questions require independent queries, the results of the first query are selected as the source data for the second query, rather than selecting the original table.

✔ Make sure that you select the source data appropriate to the task you are completing. This often means that you need to change the source data back to being the original table. Don't leave the result of the previous query as your source data.

Extracting summary data and performing calculations

Selecting summary data does not show each data item when the query is run, it can be found in Summary options when using the query wizard. This option is only available if you have selected one or more numeric fields as summary calculations cannot be completed on other data types. These allow you to perform calculations like sum and average on these numeric fields and counting the number of records.

You can also use arithmetic operations or numeric functions to perform calculations in a field where the results are calculated as the query is run. Some of the functions available for this are:

Sum – the total value of the data selected
Avg – the mean value or average of the data selected
Min – the minimum value of the data selected
Max – the maximum or largest value of the data selected
Count – the number of records selected.

You will need to remember the syntax for formulae used in your queries. If a calculated field is required (this is usually worded as 'calculated at run-time') it must have the following syntax:

NameOfTheNewCalculatedField: [ExistingFieldname] Operator [ExistingFieldname]

or

NameOfTheNewCalculatedField: [ExistingFieldname] Operator Variable

Sample exam question

Using fields from the Meals database table on page 127, identify what would be entered to:

a Create a new field called Total_Cost which is calculated at run-time. This field will show the Meal_Cost multiplied by the number of Guests. [2]

b Create a new field called Total_Plus_1 which is calculated at run-time. This field will show the Meal_Cost multiplied by the number of Guests multiplied by 2. [3]

Student's answers

a Total_Cost: [Meal_Cost] * [Guest]
b Total_Plus_1: [Meal_Cost] * [Guests] * 2

Examiner's comments

a The student has gained three of the 4 marks. The correct field selection has been made for Total_Cost and the syntax of the ':'colon after it is correct. The [Meal_Cost] field is correct and enclosed in square brackets to indicate it is a field. The correct mathematical operator (the '*') has been used, but the student has called the last field Guest rather than Guests although the square brackets are correct to indicate it is a field.

b This is the correct answer and is worth all 3 marks.

Producing reports

When an examination question asks you to produce a report it does not always mean a report generated from *Microsoft Access*. This is often the easiest method but reports can be produced in a word processor, cutting and pasting the data from other places.

When creating reports in *Access*, make sure that you show all the data in the report; often students include all the fields and correct records but do not enlarge the control (often for the data but sometimes for the label) so that all of the data for every record is fully visible. Use the drag handle on the control to enlarge it when you are in Design view.

Examiner's tips

• Look at the query (or table) used to create the report and identify the longest data item for each field. Use these data items to check in the report that each control is wide enough.

• If the question does not specify the page orientation, set this to landscape to allow more data to fit across each page.

Sorting data

Data can be sorted in either the query or the report. At IGCSE level it is easier to sort the data in the report. At this level you do not need to use grouping within your reports. Here are two examples of data being sorted in ascending order:

apple	or	1
ball		2
cake		3
dog		4

129

Cambridge IGCSE ICT Study and Revision Guide © Graham Brown and David Watson, 2017

Here are two examples of data being sorted in descending order:

dog
cake
ball
apple

or

4
3
2
1

Exam-style questions

1 Describe the following database features:

   a A record

   b A field

   c A file

   d A table

   e A report

   f A query

   g A calculated control   [7 marks]

2 Explain the differences between a flat-file database and a relational database.   [4 marks]

3 My-Music-Inc sells many music DVDs. Below is a small selection of the DVDs stored on its database.

   The data has been sorted on two fields.

Artist	Album	Released	Price	Tracks
Little Mix	Glory Days	2016	£10.00	12
Scorpions	Return to Forever	2015	£10.00	12
Elvis	The Wonder of You	2016	£10.00	14
Emile Sande	Long Live the Angels	2016	£7.00	15
Phil Collins	The Singles	2016	£7.00	16
Michael Buble	Nobody But Me	2016	£6.00	13
Donna Summer	The Ultimate Collection	2003	£6.00	19

   a Write down the field which was used as the primary sort in the database and the order in which it was sorted.   [2 marks]

   b Write down the field which was used as the secondary sort in the database and the order in which it was sorted.   [2 marks]

   c Tracy is the owner of My-Music-Inc and receives requests from customers about the music DVDs that are in stock. She converts these requests into search criteria.

     For example: a customer might ask for a list of DVDs that were released before 2016 and DVDs with more than 12 tracks. Tracy would write this as:

     Released < 2016 OR Tracks > 12

     Write down the search criteria for a customer who wants a list of all the DVDs that were released after 2015 that cost less than £10.00.   [3 marks]

   d Write down the names of the artists whose DVDs match the requirements of part c.   [1 mark]

Presentations

Key objectives

The objectives of this chapter are to revise:

- presentations, media and audience
- master slides
- presentation slides
- audience notes
- presenter notes
- transitions
- animations.

● Key terms

Term	Definition
Aspect ratio	The relationship between the width and height of an object. In the case of a presentation the width and height of the display, often either 4:3 or 16:9.

Presentations, media and audience

Figure 19.1 Presentation slides and audience

A presentation is a series of slides used to give information to an audience. Methods of delivery can include on a:

- large screen to teach/lecture
- monitor as a constant on-screen carousel.

They are often used to:

- give information/teach
- advertise products.

Depending on the purpose of the presentation and the target audience for the presentation, you can select the:

- type of presentation
- medium for delivery
- aspect ratio of the presentation (often 4:3 or 16:9)
- styles used within the presentation.

Keep it simple and be consistent when creating your presentation using:

- one theme
- one simple colour scheme with good contrast
- one or two font styles
- consistent font sizes
- bulleted lists rather than sentences
- a master slide.

Master slides

A master slide allows you to design/change the layout of all slides with one action. It holds information on colours, fonts, effects and the positioning of objects on the slides. Adding or changing master slide elements means that you do not have to change every slide individually.

To change all slides in *Microsoft PowerPoint* always change the settings in the primary (top) master slide. This one overrides the slide masters for the other slide types which are found below the primary master slide.

Presentation slides

Check carefully as you place objects on each slide that no object touches or overlaps the objects placed on the master slide (unless instructed to do so by the question paper). Make sure that the objects are clearly visible and that the text has good contrast with the colours in the background/theme you have selected.

Different types of slide layout will allow you to place text, images, lines, shapes, graphs and charts, video and audio clips on the slide. Select carefully the type of slide that you require each time you insert a new slide.

Audience notes

If a presentation is being used to teach or lecture to an audience, it is common for audience notes to be used. These are paper copies of the slides of a presentation that are given to the audience, so they can add their own notes and take them away from the presentation. If you are required to print audience notes in *PowerPoint,* select the appropriate option from the 'Handout' section.

Presenter notes

Presenter notes are also used when teaching or lecturing to an audience. Presenter notes are a copy of the presentation's slides with prompts and/or key facts that need to be told to the audience by the person delivering the presentation. Presenter notes are added in the Notes area of the presentation, just below the slides. If you are required to print presenter notes in *PowerPoint,* selecting 'Notes Pages' is often the most appropriate.

Transitions

Transitions between slides are the methods used to introduce/move to a new slide. This can be simply replacing the existing slide with a new slide or using a number of different features to change from one to another. Transitions can be timed to run automatically (for example, in a looped on-screen carousel) or set to be manually selected by clicking the mouse (a controlled presentation). For the practical examinations, always use the same transition throughout the presentation (unless told otherwise in the question paper). Use screen shots to show the examiner that you have used transitions, by selecting the Slide Sorter view, then the Transitions tab.

Animations

An animation effect is the effect used to introduce an object within the slide. Animations can be timed or manually selected by clicking the mouse. For the practical examinations, always use the same animation throughout the presentation (unless told otherwise in the question paper). Use screen shots of the Animation Pane to show the examiner your animations.

Sample exam question

Discuss the statement:

'Sarah says "Transitions and animations in a presentation are the same thing", but Brian disagrees.'   [6]

Cambridge IGCSE ICT Study and Revision Guide © Graham Brown and David Watson, 2017

Student's answer

Brian is right because they are not the same thing.

Examiner's comments

This is a really weak answer, there is no evidence presented to the examiner why the student thinks that Brian is correct. As a 'discuss' question arguments for and against would be expected; in this case, it would be a good idea to suggest that they are both very similar as they are 'actions' that are performed on slides and the objects placed on slides. The student could enhance this by saying that both actions can be timed to run automatically or to operate when the mouse is clicked. These factors would support Sarah's argument. However, transitions are actions performed on the slides whereas animations are on objects within the slides, which would support Brian's argument. A reasoned conclusion from these points would also allow the student to gain an extra mark.

> **Examiner's tip**
>
> Do not give a short one-line answer to answer any 'discuss' question. Always look for two sides to the discussion, offering different points and detail to support these points for both sides before trying to use the points to come up with a reasoned conclusion.

Exam-style questions

1 A presentation will be delivered as a lecture and use both presenter notes and audience notes. Explain why audience notes and presenter notes often contain different content. [2 marks]

2 A presentation will be used in a shopping mall to advertise different shops and their products. Identify the feature added to the presentation to make sure that it never ends. [1 mark]

CHAPTER 20 — Data analysis

Key objectives

The objectives of this chapter are to revise:

- data models
- spreadsheet structures
- formulae
- absolute and relative cell referencing
- functions
- nested functions
- test the data model
- select subsets of data
- sort data
- format cells.

● Key terms

Term	Definition
Cell	A single square/box within a spreadsheet, into which only a single entry can be placed.
Row	All the cells in one horizontal line in a spreadsheet.
Column	All the cells in one vertical line in a spreadsheet.
Sheet	All the cells in one two-dimensional grid within a spreadsheet workbook.
Label	Text placed in a spreadsheet cell, often denoting a heading or name associated with a value.
Value	A number placed in a spreadsheet cell.
Formula	A set of instructions/calculation placed in a spreadsheet cell. The result of the calculation is usually displayed in the cell. A formula can include cell references, numbers, mathematical symbols and, in some cases, pre-defined functions.
Function	Is a pre-set formula with a name (which is a reserved word) placed in a spreadsheet cell.
Absolute reference	Is a cell reference within a formula that will not change when a cell is replicated. To set this, a $ symbol is placed before the part of the cell reference that must not change.
Relative reference	A cell reference within a formula that will change when a cell is replicated.
Range	A group or block of cells in a spreadsheet that have been selected or highlighted.
Named cell	A cell that is given a more meaningful name by the user than its usual cell reference.
Named range	A group or block of cells in a spreadsheet that have been given a single name by the user. This allows the user to enter this name in their formulae rather than remembering the cell references for the cells in this range.
Nested functions	One spreadsheet function is used within another function in a cell.
Spreadsheet model	A spreadsheet that is used to investigate different outcomes by changing one or more variables within it.
Normal data	Data used to test a system. Data that is within an acceptable range and is usual for the situation.
Abnormal data	Data used to test a system. Data that is of the wrong type (for example, text where it should be numeric) or is outside the accepted range.
Extreme data	Data used to test a system. Where data must be within a certain range, extreme data is the data on either boundary of the range.

Data models

A spreadsheet is often used to create a data model. By changing the contents of one or more cells in a spreadsheet, different outcomes can be calculated and predicted. Sometimes data modelling is called making a 'what if scenario'.

Cambridge IGCSE ICT Study and Revision Guide © Graham Brown and David Watson, 2017

These models are often:

- financial
- mathematical
- scientific.

Spreadsheet structures

A spreadsheet is a two-dimensional table or grid consisting of rows, columns and cells and is used to perform calculations.

All spreadsheets store data using:

Rows Each row is all the cells in one horizontal line in a spreadsheet. The row heading contains the number displayed to the left of the first cell.

Columns Each column is all the cells in one vertical line in a spreadsheet. The column heading contains the letter displayed above the top cell.

Cells Each is a single square/box within a spreadsheet into which only a single entry can be placed. A cell can hold a:

- label (some text)
- number
- formula (that starts with an = sign).

Cells can be formatted to display data in different ways, so what a user sees in the cell is not always the actual content of the cell.

Each cell has a reference like C5 which is the cell's address in the spreadsheet. You can give an individual cell or a block of cells a name, so a cell's reference may not be seen if the cell has been given a name. These cells or blocks of cells are called named cells and named ranges.

Sometimes more than one spreadsheet (which is sometimes called a worksheet) are stored together in a workbook.

Examiner's tip

Practise using named cells and named ranges. These are often required in the practical examinations. Make sure that you name the range exactly as it appears in the question paper (including case).

Formulae

Formulae start with an = sign. Simple formulae can be used to:

- Refer to the contents of another cell. For example: cell A2 contains the formula =B4
  The formula copies the contents of B4 and displays it in A2. If the contents of B4 were changed, then the contents of A2 would also change.
- Perform calculations. For example: cell A7 contains the formula =A5+A6
  The formula adds together the contents of cells A5 and A6 and displays the result in cell A7. If the values held in either A5 or A6 were changed, then the contents of A7 would change.

The spreadsheet performs all calculations using the mathematical order of operations. It always performs anything in brackets (or parentheses) first, then indices (or powers), Multiplication, Division, Addition and finally Subtraction last.

Mathematical operators

Symbol	Operation
+	Addition
–	Subtraction
*	Multiplication
/	Division
^	Indices (to the power of)

Sample exam questions

Nicola tries the following formulae in her spreadsheet to model the total cost of some items:

	A	B	C
1	Number of items	Cost per item	
2	5	6	
3			
4	Total cost		
5	=5*6		
6	=A2*B2		

a Calculate the answers that will be seen in:

  i Cell A5

  ii Cell A6 [2]

b Explain, giving examples, why these two formulae might not always provide the same answers. [3]

Student's answers

a i 30
  ii 30
b Both give the same answer so they are both correct.

Examiner's comments

Both parts of part a of this question are correct. For part b, this is very short answer for a 3 mark question, and it contains an incorrect response as it ignores the help from the question suggesting the formulae 'might not always provide the same answers'. Although the student has realised that for this set of data the correct answer is gained in cell A5, they have not realised that, should the number of items or the cost of each item change, this cell would still give the total 30. As the question tells us that this spreadsheet will be used to model the total cost of some items, it is almost certain that the contents of either cell A2 or B2 (or both) are likely to change. When this happens the answer in cell A6 will give the correct answer, but the formula in cell A5 is unlikely to do so. To gain the final mark for this question, the student would demonstrate this reasoning and then conclude that Nicola is not correct with her statement.

Examiner's tip

When asked to model data, design your spreadsheet so that you do not have to change your formulae. Referencing to other cells (like the formula in A6 in the question above) is the best method.

Absolute and relative cell referencing

Absolute cell referencing is a way of fixing the position of a cell within a formula. It is fixed using the $ key. For example, the formula **=A3*$A$1** has the reference to cell A1 set as an **absolute reference** while the reference to cell A3 is a **relative reference**. When the formula is replicated (copied) the reference to cell A1 will not change but the reference to cell A3 will change.

Named cells and named ranges are automatically set as absolute references.

	A	B
1	2	Times Table
2		
3	1	=A3*$A$1
4	2	=A4*$A$1
5	3	=A5*$A$1
6	4	=A6*$A$1
7	5	=A7*$A$1

Functions

A function is a pre-set formula with a name. All types of spreadsheet software contain built-in functions. Make sure you are familiar with the use of each of these functions:

Function	Use	Example
SUM	Adds two or more numbers together.	=SUM(A3:A9)
AVERAGE	Calculates the average (mean) of a range of numbers by adding all the numbers together and dividing this total by the number of numbers that were added.	=AVERAGE(A3:A9)
MAX	Displays the largest (maximum) number from a range of numbers.	=MAX(A3:A9)
MIN	Displays the smallest (minimum) number from a range of numbers.	=MIN(A3:A9)
INT	Calculates the integer (whole number) part of a number by removing all digits after the decimal point.	=INT(B3)
ROUND	Calculates a number rounded to a number of decimal places. If 0 decimal places are specified it rounds to the nearest whole number. This looks at the first digit after the decimal point and, if it is five or more, adds one to the whole number answer.	=ROUND(B3,0)
COUNT	This looks at the cells within a given range and counts the number of these cells that contain numbers.	=COUNT(A3:A9)
COUNTA	This looks at the cells within a given range and counts the number of these cells that contain labels and/or numbers.	=COUNTA(A3:A9)
COUNTIF	This looks at the cells within a given range and counts the number of cells in that range that meet a given condition. The condition is placed in the function and can be a number, a label, an inequality or a cell reference.	=COUNTIF(A3:A9,B3)
IF	This gives different actions/calculations/results depending upon the results of a given condition. If the condition is true, the first action/ calculation/result is displayed/calculated. If the condition is false the second action/calculation/ result is displayed/calculated.	=IF(A1="Fred",0.5,A2*3)
SUMIF	This looks at the cells within a given range and if the cells in that range meet a given condition it adds the value in a corresponding cell to produce the total.	=SUMIF(A3:A9,4,B3:B9)
HLOOKUP	This performs a horizontal look-up of data, by looking at each of the cells in the top row of a given range, and comparing them with a given condition. The condition is placed in the function and can be a number, a string, an inequality or a cell reference. If the condition matches the contents of a cell, a value is looked up from the corresponding cell in a row below. The number of the required row is placed in the function (in the example shown, it is the second row in the range). The final parameter of the function can be 0 (or False) which forces an exact match when the data is compared or 1 (or True) for an approximate match.	=HLOOKUP(A3,C2:G3,2,0)
VLOOKUP	This performs a vertical look-up of data, by looking at each of the cells in the left column of a given range, and comparing them with a given condition. The condition is placed in the function and can be a number, a string, an inequality or a cell reference. If the condition matches the contents of a cell, a value is looked up from the corresponding cell in a column to the right. The number of the column to the right is placed in the function (in the example shown, it is the third column in the range). The final parameter of the function can be 0 (or False) which forces an exact match when the data is compared or 1 (or True) for an approximate match.	=VLOOKUP(A3,A5:C9,3,1)

Nested functions

Sometimes examination questions will ask for formulae that are more complex. These types of question will often need one function inside another function. If three different conditions are needed then nested IF functions are ideal. If there are lots of different conditions, using either VLOOKUP or HLOOKUP is a better option than lots of different nested IF statements.

Cambridge IGCSE ICT Study and Revision Guide © Graham Brown and David Watson, 2017

Sample exam question

Identify the formula that you would place in cell A10 to display the text Lower, Middle or Higher depending upon the contents of cell A3. If cell A3 contains a value:

- between 8 and 12 inclusive then display 'Middle'
- less than 8 then display 'Lower'
- greater than 12 then display 'Higher'. [8]

Student's answer

=IF(A3<8,"Lower",IF(8=<A3=12,"Middle",IF(A3=<12Higher",0))

Examiner's comments

There is no single correct answer to this question. The student has started well by realising that nested IF functions would offer the best solution, but because there can be no other possible conditions for numbers held in A3 (it has to be less than 8, between 8 and 12 or greater than 12) only two IF statements are needed.

The student has also correctly identified that the data in the question is in an illogical order and has worked from the lowest value in A3 to the highest.

The initial =IF(A3<8,"Lower", is correct and would gain marks, but the next section contains a serious syntax error. The condition IF(8<=A3=12, would not be recognised by Excel as this contains two conditions and no logical operator like AND or OR to link them. The two conditions are not needed as anything less than 8 has already been trapped by the earlier function, so a single condition like IF(A3<=12 would work. Because Excel would stop at this point, no further marks would be awarded for this formula.

This student's solution also contains another syntax error. There are three opening brackets and only two closing brackets.

There are many correct possible answers, such as:

=IF(A3<8,"Lower",IF(A3<=12,"Middle","Higher"))
=IF(A3>12,"Higher",IF(A3>=8,"Middle", "Lower"))

> **Examiner's tip**
> When given a question that requires nested IF functions, always work from lowest to highest (in order) or from highest to lowest. Do *not* assume that the order of the question will give you the correct results.

Test the data model

Create a test plan. The test plan should test each formula entered into your spreadsheet. The first part of the test plan, the expected output, must be completed before the formulae are entered into the spreadsheet. Choose numbers that are easy to calculate with, and numbers that test every boundary as appropriate test data. Include (where possible) at least two examples of normal, abnormal and extreme data. This test data must be selected to test each calculation. The results of each calculation for each piece of data should be calculated manually (performed without the spreadsheet) and recorded in the expected output column of the test plan.

Enter the formulae, then enter each item of test data from the test plan into your spreadsheet and record the actual output for this data in your test plan. Compare your expected results to the actual results. This should help you identify any errors. Make sure that you test each element of the spreadsheet with normal, abnormal and, where appropriate, extreme data.

Cambridge IGCSE ICT Study and Revision Guide © Graham Brown and David Watson, 2017

At the end of this process another test can be undertaken using 'live data'. This is real data where the results are already known (perhaps from the previous month's figures from a previous system) and the expected and actual results from the new system are again compared.

Select subsets of data

Use the Custom AutoFilter tool (see page 352 in the Cambridge IGCSE ICT Coursebook) to search for subsets of data in your spreadsheet. This tool will allow you to present the examiner with evidence of your method by taking screen shots of the Custom AutoFilter window and placing this in your Evidence Document. Using the dropdown filter options does not always show the examiner evidence of your method. This facility also allows you to use other features, like the use of the ? symbol to show a single wildcard character and the * symbol to show a wildcard selection of any length.

Sort data

Make sure that you select all the data for each item to be sorted. Make sure that you do not include the column headings in the data that is sorted.

● Common errors

✖ When a block of data needs to be sorted into a particular order, for example, by name only, the single column of data that you are sorting by (the name column) has been selected.

✔ Highlight the whole block of data before performing the sort. Otherwise, when the data is sorted (by name column) the other data in the block would not be sorted with it and the integrity of the data would be lost.

✖ When all the data has been selected the column headings are also selected so that these are sorted within the data.

✔ Highlight all the data apart from the column headings or select the tick box for 'My data has headers'.

> **Examiner's tip**
> If more than one level of sorting is required on your data, always use 'Custom Sort...' to open the sort window. This allows you to add the different levels of sorting and also allows you to screen shot this window to place evidence of your method in your Evidence Document.

Format cells

Cells can be formatted to enhance the contents and create, for example, titles and subtitles. Make sure to practise merging cells, applying bold, italic and underlining, changing the background and foreground (text) colours, selecting different font sizes and styles, including serif and sans serif fonts.

Formatting cells containing numbers changes the way each cell is displayed but does not change the value held within it.

● Common errors

✖ Where a question states 'Calculate... to 0 decimal places'; you format the cell(s) as integers (to 0 decimal places) rather than using the INT or ROUND functions.

✔ If the question states 'Calculate... to 0 decimal places' use the INT or ROUND function.

● Common errors

✖ Currency format is applied to all numeric cells in the spreadsheet.
✔ Check what each cell represents. Only format it as currency or percentage, and so on, if it contains that type of data.
✖ The currency symbol can't be found in my regional settings so I will not format the cells.
✔ Scroll down the list of currencies available until the three-letter ISO codes appear. If the currency symbol for the country is not available use the ISO (international standard) code, for example: for US dollars ($) it is USD, for pounds (£) sterling it is GBP (Great Britain pounds).

Change the size of the row and columns
Make sure that you set the column width and row height so that all data and labels are fully displayed.

● Common errors

✖ Producing printouts, particularly formulae printouts, where not all of the formulae are fully visible. If examiners cannot see what you have done, they cannot award you the marks!
✔ Check that each formula is fully visible. Don't just check the first row. Often the last row is much longer than the first. If it can't all be seen, make the row wider.
✖ Producing printouts where all the formulae are fully visible but are so small it is impossible to read.
✔ Do not leave lots of white space in each cell after the formulae. If the question paper does not instruct you to print on a single page wide, allow the formulae printout to run over more than one page.

Cambridge IGCSE ICT Study and Revision Guide © Graham Brown and David Watson, 2017

Exam-style questions

1 The following spreadsheet shows the value of sales in a number of countries.

	A	B	C	D	E	F	G	H	I
1	**Country**	**Code**		**Currency**	**Value**		**Date**	**Code**	**Sales**
2	Brazil	BR		Real (R$)	940.00		15/12/2016	EC	200.50
3	Canada	CA		Dollar ($)	2050.50		16/12/2016	CA	320.20
4	Colombia	CO		Peso	62000.00		16/12/2016	PA	155.00
5	Ecuador	EC		Dollar ($)	746.50		17/12/2016	CO	12000.00
6	Mexico	MX		Peso	7650.00		18/12/2016	PA	200.00
7	Panama	PA		Balboa	885.00		20/12/2016	VZ	350.00
8	Venezuela	VZ		Bolivar	350.00		04/01/2017	EC	400.50
9							05/01/2017	CA	1020.00
10							09/01/2017	CO	30000.00
11							09/01/2017	MX	3150.00
12							10/01/2017	MX	2400.00
13							10/01/2017	PA	320.00
14							10/01/2017	BR	1210.50
15							11/01/2017	BR	940.00
16							12/01/2017	PA	210.00
17							14/01/2017	MX	2100.00
18							15/01/2017	CA	310.00
19							15/01/2017	CA	400.20
20							15/01/2017	CO	20000.00
21							16/01/2017	EC	145.50
22							No. products =		20.00

  a Cell E5 contains the formula:

  =SUMIF($H$2:$H$21,B5,$I$2:$I$21)

  Explain what this formula does. [4 marks]

  b Write down the formula you would expect to see in cell E6. [3 marks]

  c The formula in cell I22 refers to all the values in column I. Write down the formula you would expect to see in cell I22 to produce the value **20**. [2 marks]

2 Two students use different formulae to calculate the whole number of dollars for products that they have sold.

Student A uses the formula:

=INT(A42*A43)

Student B uses the formula:

=ROUND(A42*A43,0)

Explain (using examples) why sometimes the two formulae give the same answer, other times they do not. [4 marks]

3 a A cell contains the function =COUNTIF(ObjectTable,$A$3)

  Explain what this function does. [3 marks]

  b Explain why $A$3 has been used rather than A3. [3 marks]

Cambridge IGCSE ICT Study and Revision Guide © Graham Brown and David Watson, 2017

Website authoring

Key objectives

The objectives of this chapter are to revise:

- web page creation layers
- web page structure
- styles in HTML
- tables
- images in a web page
- animated images, video and audio files
- bulleted and numbered lists
- hyperlinks
- stylesheet structure
- working with colour
- text in the stylesheet
- background colours and images
- classes
- tables in the stylesheet
- publish a website
- test a website.

● Key terms

Term	Definition
Website	A collection of interrelated web pages that relate to one topic or organisation and are usually accessible via the internet.
Content layer	One of the three layers in web page development. The content layer is used to define the structure of the web page, often using tables or frames, and the content of the pages including text or images and hyperlinks to other pages. The content layer is often written in HTML or XHTML.
Presentation layer	One of the three layers in web page development. The presentation layer is used to define how a web page will look to the viewer. It provides the colour schemes, themes and styles seen when a web page is displayed and is usually written in CSS.
Behaviour layer	One of the three layers in web page development. The behaviour layer is used to do 'an action' (rather than just display or link to other pages) and often uses script languages embedded into the HTML. There are many different script languages but the most common for web development are JavaScript PHP, Perl and CGI.
HTML	HyperText Markup Language: a text-based language used to create markup, so that web browser software will be able to display information in different ways.
CSS	Cascading StyleSheet: a language used for the presentation layer in web development. This language is used to define how elements of a web page appear in the web browser. CSS elements can be embedded within HTML or attached to a web page as a cascading stylesheet.
Text editor	Software that allows you to type and edit plain text. It contains few or no features that allow formatting of documents.
WYSIWYG	What You See Is What You Get: in terms of website authoring, relates to packages that create or edit HTML markup using a graphics interface. For example, you may enlarge or reduce the size of an image on a web page by using the drag handles. The WYSIWYG package will edit the HTML markup so that this change will appear whenever the page is opened.
Tag	A command used in HTML to instruct a web browser how to display text, images or other objects. The tags are not displayed on the web page. Some tags are used with attributes.
Head	The section of HTML in a web page that contains page titles (visible in the browser tab but not on the page), styles (for example, the links to external stylesheets), and the meta data (for example, the tags used by search engines).
Body	The section of HTML in a web page that contains the contents (for example, text, images) and the tags describing the content, hyperlinks and structure (for example, tables used to lay out the page) of a web page.
Ordered list	A list within a web page that is ordered and has numbers or letters for each list item.

Unordered list	A list within a web page that is in no specific order and has bullet points for each list item.
Hyperlink	A reference within an electronic document (like a web page) to another place in the same document or to a different document. Hyperlinks are the foundation of any hypertext system, including the world wide web.
Embedded styles	Styles (created in CSS) that are inserted and saved within the body section of the HTML of a web page.
Attached stylesheet	A document containing style definitions that is attached to a web page using the link tag in the head section. The styles from this stylesheet are used to display the web page.
RGB	Defines the different amounts of red, green and blue (which are the primary colours of light) that are sent to the display to change the colour of each pixel.
Bandwidth	This is a reference to the range of frequencies a communication channel can handle. The bigger the bandwidth the more data can be sent and received at the same time. The amount of data that can be communicated also relies upon the transfer rate. This is often used to describe internet connection, with the term 'broadband' meaning it has more than 3KHz (although in real terms at least 300MHz is needed in current systems).
Domain name	This is the name given to the place we can find a particular website on the internet.
FTP	File Transfer Protocol allows a copy of data to be sent from one computer to another. It controls the data and sends it in blocks, checking each block as it arrives for errors.

Web page creation layers

A web page is created using three layers:

- **The content layer** – contains the structure of the web page and its contents including text, images and hyperlinks. This is created in HTML (HyperText Markup Language).
- **The presentation layer** – contains the styles and appearance of the web page. This is created in CSS (Cascading StyleSheet).
- **The behaviour layer** – contains actions within the web page that often involve script languages. This is often created in JavaScript but is beyond the scope of the IGCSE course.

Web page structure

This is completed in the content layer and is created in HTML. Whether you use a text editor like *Notepad* or a What You See Is What You Get (WYSIWYG) package to develop a web page, it is always wise to add comments to your page. For the practical examination, these should include your name, centre number and candidate number. Comments are added using the following HTML syntax:

```
<!--This is a comment in html -->
```

Make sure your HTML5 starts with `<!DOCTYPE html>` followed by `<html>` and ends with `</html>`.

Between the `<html>` and `</html>` tags, each web page is split into two sections:

- the head section
- the body section.

The head section is always above the body section and contains elements used in the page but not displayed on the page, for example, the page title and attached stylesheets. The body section contains the structure of the page, the contents placed within this structure and any hyperlinks. The structure of the web page you will create for the examinations will use tables.

Examiner's tip

Each time you make a small change to your HTML (or your CSS), save it, load the web page back into your browser (or press F5 to refresh it), then test the changes you have made. If you save and test after each change, it is easy to correct any errors that you may make.

Styles in HTML

HTML contains a number of pre-defined styles, including:

- p   paragraph style
- li   list style (for bulleted or numbered lists)
- h1   heading style 1 (usually has the largest font size)
- h2   heading style 2
- h3   heading style 3
- h4   heading style 4
- h5   heading style 5
- h6   heading style 6 (usually has the smallest font size)

Your browser has default settings defined for each of these styles but you can change how each one looks later in the presentation layer. Each of these styles is applied with an opening tag such as `<p>` and closed with `</p>`. The / tells the browser that this style has now finished. When you define any text in your web page always use one of the style definitions above.

Tables

Tables are used to structure the web page. They are used to organise page layout and often to define the structure with no borders visible, so that a page keeps a similar look even when a browser is resized. Each table can have a header with header data, footer with footer data, and body section with table rows and table data in each cell. These areas are defined by the tags `<table>`, `<thead>`, `<th>`, `<tfoot>`, `<tbody>`, `<tr>`, `<td>`, respectively. Again a / is placed after the < to close each section, for example `</table>`.

Table borders can be set as on using the attribute `<table border="1">` or off with `<table border="">`. They can also be made invisible in the presentation layer (CSS) attached to the web page. All other changes to table borders are made in the CSS, although this is sometimes placed in the HTML as an embedded style using the style attribute. An example of this is to merge all borders within a table where the CSS border-collapse element has been embedded in the HTML: `<table border="1" style="border-collapse:collapse">`.

See page 373 of the Cambridge IGCSE ICT Coursebook for more detail on table structures.

Examiner's tip

Practise creating and editing tables including the use of the rowspan and colspan attributes `<td rowspan=…>` and `<td colspan=…>` to make table data appear over more than one row and/or column.

Sample exam question

Identify the HTML used to create a table structure, with no formatting, to look like this:

Cost table	
Item	Cost
Apple	$0.40
Banana	$0.80

List only the HTML for the table and one line of markup as a comment with your name. [6]

Student's answer

```
<!-- Graham Brown, table for sample question -->
<table border="1" style="border-width:2px">
 <tr>
  <td rowspan="2">
   <p>Cost table</p>
  </td>
 </tr>
 <tr>
  <td>
   <p>Item</p>
  </td>
  <td>
   <p>Cost</p>
  </td>
 </tr>
 <tr>
  <td>
   <p>Apple</p>
  </td>
  <td>
   <p>$0.40</p>
  </td>
 </tr>
  <td>
   <p>Banana</p>
  </td>
  <td>
   <p>$0.80</p>
  </td>
 </tr>
```

Examiner's comments

This markup contains a number of errors that would not allow the table to be displayed as shown in the question. The table data in the first row contains an error. This should show a colspan set to 2 rather than a rowspan set to 2. The final row of the table does not have a `<tr>` tag. The table has not been closed with a `</table>` tag. The markup for the table tag contains embedded CSS using the style attribute. The indented markup helps both the student and the examiner check each pair of tags is present, notice how all `<tr>` and `</tr>` tags start at the same point on each line and within each table row all the `<td>` tags also start from the same point but are indented from the `<tr>` tags.

Cambridge IGCSE ICT Study and Revision Guide © Graham Brown and David Watson, 2017

Images in a web page

Images are inserted into the framework of the table. The image (`<img>`) tag is used for this. This tag should always have (at least) two attributes, these are the:

- image source (`src`) which identifies the name of the file that will be used as the image
- the alternate text (`alt`) which is displayed instead of the image if the image cannot be displayed.

The image tag is one of the few tags that does not have a closing tag. An example of the syntax is:

```
<img src="img0047.jpg" alt="Image of a computer monitor">
```

You will notice that the image source does not have any file path. For this hyperlink to work, the image *must* be stored in the same folder as the saved web page (they will be uploaded from this folder to the host web server) or the image will not be displayed.

Bitmap graphics formats have always been used for websites, in particular JPEG (.jpg), GIF (.gif) and more recently PNG (.png). Scalable vector graphics (.svg) are now also being used in some web pages but these are not suitable for all types of image.

For the purposes of the IGCSE, concentrate your answers on bitmap format graphics (not .bmp format) such as JPEGs, GIFs and PNGs. Each of these can be resized in a graphics package (often to reduce the image and file sizes) or you can use embedded CSS in a style attribute of the image tag. So to resize the image img0047 to 200 pixels wide (and maintain its aspect ratio) the example shown above will change to:

```
<img src="img0047.jpg" style="width:200px" alt="Image of a
computer monitor">
```

Animated images, video and audio files

To include animated images, use an animated GIF file and insert this like a still image above, or use the `<video>` tag then add width and height attributes for the video size and controls if required. A `<source>` tag is used to identify the source of the video, which is different to the attribute used for a still image or animated GIF file. An example of the syntax used for a video file is:

```
<video width="300" height="224" controls>
  Your browser does not support this type of video.
  <source src="wreck.mp4" type="video/mp4">
</video>
```

Audio files are placed in the HTML in a very similar way to video files, but do not need width and height attributes. For example:

```
<audio controls>
  Your browser does not support this type of audio file.
  <source src="whale.mp3" type="audio/mpeg">
</audio>
```

Bulleted and numbered lists

The `<li>` tag is used to open each item in a list, and each item is closed with `</li>` tag. There are two types of lists available in a web page:

- An **ordered list** (which can appear as a numbered or lettered list). Each ordered list (not each list item) starts with the `<ol>` tag and ends with `</ol>`.
- An **unordered list** (which is a bulleted list). Each unordered list (not each list item) starts with the `<ul>` tag and the list ends with `</ul>`.

Sample exam question

The following HTML will be placed in the body section of a web page.

```
<h1>Holiday destinations</h1>
<ul>
  <li>Maldives</li>
    <ol>
      <li>relaxing beach holidays</li>
      <li>scuba diving</li>
      <li>wind surfing</li>
    </ol>
  <li>Austria</li>
    <ol>
      <li>skiing</li>
      <li>climbing</li>
      <li>mountain biking</li>
    </ol>
  <li>Iceland</li>
</ul>
```

Describe the results of this markup when seen in a web browser. [6]

Student's answer

The title Holiday destinations has been placed above nested lists. There are three lists, one main list and two sub-lists.

Examiner's comments

This is the beginning of a good answer. The student has identified that the initial text is in style h1 and is, therefore, a heading (although it would have been better for them to also describe this to the examiner). They have also identified that there are three lists, one a main list and two sub-lists.

The student has not identified the types of list used. For example: 'The main list is a bulleted or unordered list. It is not possible to identify the type of bullet points that would be seen because that depends upon the list styles applied in the stylesheet or on the browser's default list style setting.'

For the two sub-lists the student could identify 'that for two of the countries a numbered or lettered list of some popular activities that take place in the country has been included. It is not possible to identify the format of these lists from the HTML as the presentation elements are covered in the stylesheet or in the browser's default ordered list settings'. Another good method is to use a diagram as an example, along with the text, for example: 'The browser may display this so it looks like the example shown here.' This could then lead into further detail like that the sub-lists are indented from the main list, and so on. As it is a 6 mark question detail is required.

Holiday destinations

- Maldives
  1. relaxing beach holidays
  2. scuba diving
  3. wind surfing
- Austria
  1. skiing
  2. climbing
  3. mountain biking
- Iceland

> **Examiner's tip**
> While a diagram can help answer a question, the description is what will gain the marks although sometimes a sketched diagram can help to make it clear to the examiner what you are describing.

● Hyperlinks

A hyperlink is a method of accessing another document or resource from your current application. Hyperlinks can:

- move your position within a page
- open another page, either locally or on the internet
- open your email editor so that you can compose an email.

Each hyperlink is created using an `<a>` (anchor tag) and closed with `</a>`. These tags must surround the text or image that will be used for the hyperlink. The hyperlink is created by adding an `href` (hyperlink reference) attribute to the anchor, which shows the place to move to (or action to perform). If the `href` is set to a file path, for example: `<a href="page33.htm">` this must be a relative file path (containing no references to any folder structure or local drives).

The use of an absolute file path, for example: `<a href="D:/myfiles/page33.htm">` may work on the machine you are using but is unlikely to work when uploaded to your web server.

Hyperlinks can be used to open web pages in the same browser window or a new browser window by setting the `target` attribute. The target attribute can be attached to an individual hyperlink like this: `<a href="page33.htm" target="_blank">`

There are a small number of acceptable target extensions but for IGCSE `_blank` opens the new web page or document in a new window or tab and `_self` opens it in the current window or tab.

If all hyperlinks to linked web pages or documents are to appear the same, then this attribute can be set in the attached stylesheet as a default target window using: `<base target="_blank">`

This *must* be placed in the `<head>` section of the web page. If the target attribute is not used, the browser will decide where to open a web page.

Sample exam questions

a Describe what the following HTML does. [2]

```
<a href="#mb1">mountain biking</a>
```

b Explain why the HTML in part a may not work. [1]

c Describe what the following HTML does. [2]

```
<a href=https://www.hoddereducation.co.uk/ target="_blank">
<img src="bk.jpg" alt=""></a>
```

d Describe what the following HTML does. [2]

```
<a href="mailto:graham.a.brown@hotmail.co.uk?subject=Revision
%20guide">here</a>
```

Cambridge IGCSE ICT Study and Revision Guide © Graham Brown and David Watson, 2017

Student's answers

a When the user clicks on the text 'mountain biking' they are moved to an internal bookmark which has been called 'mb1'.

b It is not there.

c This hyperlink moves the user from the image called 'bk.jpg'. When it is clicked on it goes to a website.

d This sends an email to the person with the address graham.a.brown@hotmail.co.uk.

Examiner's comments

a Is a sound student answer worth both marks, the first for identifying that the text is used for the link and for identifying that it moves the user to an internal anchor. It would have been even better if the student had used the word 'hyperlink' in their response.

b This is a common type of answer. The response is not worth any marks because the student does not explain what is not there. A response like 'There may be no internal bookmark called "mb1" within the body text of the web page' would gain this mark.

c This response starts well. The student has identified it is a hyperlink and has been very specific about the image and named it. The second part of this response is not as strong; the student has identified that it goes to a website but has not been specific enough in their answer. There is also no mention of the target window selected in this markup. This new web page would open in a new window called '_blank' and would, therefore, appear as a new tab in the browser.

d This is a classic incorrect answer. The hyperlink does not send an email. When the hyperlink is clicked on it opens your default email editor and prepares an email to the recipient. In this example, it also places the text 'Revision guide' into the subject line of the email, the %20 forces a single space between the words.

> **Examiner's tip**
> Think carefully about the answers you give, for 'describe' questions give the examiner as much detail as possible. Do not assume the examiner knows what you are thinking … put it down in your answer.

Stylesheet structure

This is completed in the presentation layer and is created in CSS. Whether you use a text editor like *Notepad* or a WYSIWYG package to develop a web page, it is always wise to add comments to your stylesheet. For the practical examination, these should include your name, centre number and candidate number. Comments are added using the following HTML syntax:

```
/* This is a comment in css */
```

Styles can be applied by using:

- embedded styles, where styles are placed using a style attribute within the HTML, but these have to be defined for each element
- attached stylesheets, where styles are placed in a document that is loaded by the browser. The style definitions from the document are applied to all elements on the web page.

Embedded styles over-rule attached styles and are placed in the HTML like this:

```
<table style="background-color: #0000ff; color: #ff0000">
```

In this example this table would have a blue background colour and yellow text, which may be different from the styles set in the attached stylesheet.

Attached stylesheets contain all the styles that may be needed for a web page. Using these saves a lot of work as the styles only need defining once, then the stylesheet can be attached to a number of pages. These web pages will then all have the same presentation features. This is very useful for showing corporate house styles. A number of different stylesheets can be attached in the `<head>` section of each web page. The bottom stylesheet has the highest priority, then the one above it, and so on, hence the name 'cascading' stylesheets as each one flows towards the bottom (like a series of cascading waterfalls, the last one being the largest and most powerful). The stylesheet is attached like this:

```
<link rel="stylesheet" href="style1.css">
```

The hyperlink reference must be a relative file path containing no references to any folder structure or local drives. If not, the stylesheet is unlikely to be found when uploaded to your web server, unless the computer using the web page has an identical filename and file structure to your computer.

If both attached stylesheets and embedded styles are included on a web page, the embedded styles override the attached stylesheet.

All CSS rules have a selector and a declaration block like this:

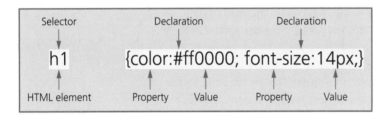

- Each element has one or more declarations, each separated by a semi-colon.
- Each declaration has a property name and a value, separated by a colon.
- Each declaration block is surrounded by curly brackets.

Examiner's tip

Practise creating styles in a stylesheet attached to a web page. Edit each style to see what difference it makes. Remember to save the stylesheet in CSS format after each change and to refresh the web page for the changes to take effect.

Working with colour

Colour is always defined in the presentation layer (using CSS), usually in an external stylesheet. Colour codes are usually referred to using hexadecimal numbers and are always listed in RGB order. RGB are the primary colours for light: Red, Green and Blue. Each hexadecimal colour code has six digits, two for red, then two for green, then two for blue. This CSS will produce a web page with a red background:

```
body    {background-color: #ff0000}
```

The # tells the browser that the number is in hexadecimal and the American spelling of color must be used. The `ff` for the red component turns on full red light for each pixel on the screen or projector and each `00` for green and blue turns off these colours. If all colours are `00` (so it becomes `#000000`) then the screen would be black as no colour is projected, and if they were all fully on (`#ffffff`) then the screen would be white as mixing red, blue and green light gives white light.

Cambridge IGCSE ICT Study and Revision Guide © Graham Brown and David Watson, 2017

Text in the stylesheet

Setting font families in your stylesheet often requires you to specify three different values for each declaration. One of these is usually a *Microsoft Windows* font, one an *Apple* font and the third is usually a generic font style in case neither of the font faces selected is available. An example of this is:

```
h1      {font-family: "Times New Roman","Times",serif}
```

The browser looks at the font list and tries to find the first named font family in its stored font list, if it is present it displays this. If not it looks at the next named font, with the same results. If none of the named fonts is available it displays its default serif or sans serif font.

Sample exam question

Define style h1 as Trebuchet, if this is not available then Trebuchet MS; if neither of these fonts is available, then the browser's default sans serif font. [4]

Student's answer

```
h1      {font-family:"Trebuchet"}
```

Examiner's comments

This student has got a font called Trebuchet installed in their computer, so they have selected this as the only font required as it works for them at that moment in time. The correct answer should have been:

```
h1      {font-family: "Trebuchet","Trebuchet MS",sans-serif}
```

Having dealt with setting font families, let us move on to consider font size. Font size can also be set when text styles are defined, for example:

```
h1      {font-family: serif; font-size: 60pt}
```

The `font-family` has been reduced to a single generic font so that it all fits on one line, and the `font-size` property value has been set to 60 points high.

Examiner's tip

Read the question carefully, especially where font size is concerned. Font sizes are likely to be specified in either points or pixels (although other types of measurement are possible). Marks are unlikely to be awarded if the correct type of measurement is not present. There must also be no space between the `60` and the `pt`.

Text alignment is set with the `text-align` property. The possible values that can be added to this are shown here:

```
h1      {text-align: left}
h2      {text-align: center}
h3      {text-align: right}
h4      {text-align: justify}
```

Text can be bold, italic or underlined. Each uses a different property for the declaration. These are:

```
h1      {font-weight:bold;
    font-style:italic;
    text-decoration:underline}
```

Cambridge IGCSE ICT Study and Revision Guide © Graham Brown and David Watson, 2017

Text can be coloured using the color property followed by a hexadecimal RGB value, such as:

```
h1      {color: #ff0000}
```

Background colour and images

Background colours and images are defined in CSS with the body selector. The background image is added with a value using url syntax like this:

```
body    {background-color:#0047fc;
         background-image: url("image3.png");
         background-repeat: no-repeat;}
```

The background repeat declaration is set to repeat if you wish to have 'tiled' images. If there is no background repeat you can define the position of the background image in the window.

Classes

Classes have been rarely used at IGCSE level, but they define different subtypes within an element. A class is defined using a dot (full stop) before the style name. Some WYSIWYG packages automatically use classes rather than defining styles. In these examples:

```
h1      {color: #ff0000}
.h1     {color: #0000ff}
```

the top line defines the style h1 and the second line defines the class h1.

● Common errors

✖ When asked to 'Create the following styles …' in a question, students generate all the correct declaration properties and values for a series of classes rather than defining the styles.

✔ When a question asks for styles, check your WYSIWYG package has not defined classes.

Tables in the stylesheet

Table definitions can be set in external stylesheets. This is very useful if web pages contain a number of tables. Different selectors can be used to format different parts of tables in different ways. For example, the body of the page, tables and table headers can have different background colours that complement each other. Table borders can also be defined in the stylesheet, for example:

```
body    {background-color:#90ee90;}
table   {background-color:#2eb757;
         border-collapse:collapse;
         border-style:solid;
         border-width:6px}
td      {border-style:solid;
         border-width:3px}
```

This defines different background colours for the table and body of the page and sets the table to have a 6-pixel-wide border around it and 3-pixel-wide gridlines within the table.

Publish a website

Websites can be hosted on your own computer or uploaded to a hosting company. Most people do not host their own websites because their internet service does not provide them with enough bandwidth. All websites have a

Cambridge IGCSE ICT Study and Revision Guide © Graham Brown and David Watson, 2017

domain name, such as www.hoddereducation.co.uk, which is used to find the site. To upload a website, file transfer protocol (FTP) is used.

Test a website

Before testing a web page you should identify its purpose and its target audience. When creating a test plan, make sure it includes both functional testing and user testing.

Functional testing checks all page elements perform as expected, including table structure, images, visibility of objects, and internal hyperlinks. This also checks if the URL works and whether all external hyperlinks work as expected.

User testing checks the website meets the purpose and is appropriate for the target audience. Users must not be IT professionals or people related to the development project (they must have no knowledge or preconceived ideas about the website). Observe, listen, but do not respond to the users.

Sample exam question

Identify **three** questions that may be asked in user testing.   [3]

Student's answer

i How easy is it to read and understand?
ii What did you like about the web page?
iii Did the website do what you expected?

Examiner's comments

The first answer is excellent, the second answer is good but contains less specific detail in the question. The first two answers have identified issues that relate to user testing. The third answer is incorrect because the user should be testing without any expectations. Other good answers include:

- What are your first impressions of the web page?
- What is the purpose of the web page?
- Was this purpose clear from the beginning?
- It there too much or little information?
- What did you dislike about the web page?

Exam-style questions

1 Explain the **three** terms:

   a http

   b web browser

   c ftp   [3 marks]

2 Explain the difference between ftp and http when dealing with files and data.   [4 marks]

Cambridge IGCSE ICT Study and Revision Guide © Graham Brown and David Watson, 2017

3 The following shows a cascading stylesheet created by a student.
It contains a number of errors. Identify each of these errors and
suggest a way to correct them.   [8 marks]

```
h1          {colour:#00006f;
             font-family:Arial,sans serif:
             font-size:20px;
             text-align:center}

h2          {colour:000040:
             font-family:Times New Roman,serif;
             font-size:24px;
             text-align:centre}

table       {border-collapse:collapse;
             border-width:6px;
             border-style:"solid";
             border-color:#004040}

td          {border-width:4px;
             border-style:solid;
             border-colour:#004040}
```

4 Describe the use of the content and presentation layers in a
web page.   [4 marks]

Cambridge IGCSE ICT Study and Revision Guide © Graham Brown and David Watson, 2017

Answers to exam-style questions

● Chapter 1

1

Computer term	Application software	System software	Operating system
managing user accounts			✓
spreadsheet software	✓		
video editing software	✓		
error handling			✓
linker		✓	
database software	✓		
device driver		✓	

2 a CLI: user types in instructions; commands must follow a precise syntax.
GUI: user uses a mouse to launch applications (using icons) or to select options from a menu.

b CLI advantages: user is in direct communication with the computer; user is not restricted to pre-determined options; it is possible to alter the computer configuration.
CLI disadvantages: a number of commands need to be learnt; it can be slow to type in commands and can be error-prone; syntax and format of each command must be exact.
GUI advantages: no need to learn any commands; more user friendly; applications can simply be launched by clicking on an icon.
GUI disadvantages: uses considerably more memory than CLI; user is limited to icons provided on screen; needs a sophisticated OS, which uses up considerable memory.

3 Laptop computer: type up his reports; send emails to his company/colleagues; surf the net to find hotel details.
Tablet: surf the net to find hotel details; keep a diary of meetings/flight times, and so on; GPS to find the way to the hotels; built-in camera to take photos of hotels and locations; can be used on the move to take notes.
Smartwatch: synchronises with his tablet; can make phone calls to the office.

4

Description	Computer term
Uses infrared light and visible light so that an object can still be seen even when it is apparently dark	night-vision enhancement (NVE)
Unmanned flying devices that can be used for army surveillance or delivering items to customers without the need for a delivery van	drones/robots
System based on the fact that photons oscillate in various directions and can be used to produce a random sequence of bits when sending data over fibre optic cables	quantum cryptography
System that uses terminology databases and translation memories to convert text written in one language into text in a different language	computer-assisted translation (CAT)
Technology that uses laser light, interference of light and diffraction of light to produce a 3-D life-like image of an object	holographic/3-D imaging
Artificial environment that uses data goggles, sensor suits, data gloves or data helmets to create 'the feeling of being there'	virtual reality
Systems used to do massive number crunching, equipped with very powerful processors and massive memories	mainframe computers

● Chapter 2

1 a keyboard
b touch screen
c scanner
d microphone
e (temperature) sensor
f graphics tablet
2 a Customer looks out for the contactless symbol:)))
Shop assistant enters amount to be paid/checkout till works out 'bill'.
Customer holds card in front of contactless reader.
System generates unique transaction number.
Message displayed on screen that payment has been accepted.

b i radio frequency identification
  ii microchip/tag; antenna; battery
  iii livestock tracking; admission passes and
    security passes; in races (for example,
    marathons) to register start and end times
    of athletes; in libraries to track books

3 a OCR: can read handwriting to allow
  extension to answers given by customers;
  poor handwriting can cause reading
  problems; requires an expensive and complex
  recognition system; needs fewer 'filling in'
  instructions for customers; less accurate and
  slower than OMR.
  OMR: uses shaded-in lozenges or lines
  joining dots; requires stored template to
  recognise position of choices; no problems
  with handwriting but marks must be made
  in designated places only; needs expensive
  and complex forms; needs more 'filling in'
  instructions; more accurate than OCR.

b

Application	MICR	Barcode reader	OMR
Reading numbers/ characters on the bottom of bank cheques (checks)	✓		
Automatically reading and marking multiple-choice question papers			✓
Allowing a fully automatic stock control system		✓	

4

Stage	Description of stage
1	D: MICR text is passed over an MICR reader
2	C: ink on the paper is first magnetised
3	B: characters are then passed over the MICR read head
4	A: as each character passes over the head it produces a unique waveform
5	E: the waveform is recognised by the computer system

5 a Uses plastic organic layers which are thinner
  and lighter than glass; can be made into any
  required shape; brighter light than normal
  LEDs; don't require any back-lighting unlike
  LCD screens; uses less power than LCDs;
  very large field of view (nearly 180°).

b Heavy and bulky; runs very hot and can be a
  fire risk; uses a lot of electricity; screens can
  often flicker.

6 Laser printers: can handle large print runs (large
  buffers); very high quality of output; toner
  cartridges last a long time; relatively cheap
  to buy; can be expensive to run (especially
  colour laser printers); produce ozone and toner
  particulates which are a potential health hazard.
  Inkjet printers: high-quality output; relatively
  cheap to buy; small footprint; small ink
  cartridges; small buffers; printing can 'smudge';
  ink tends to be very expensive; rather noisy in
  operation.
  Dot matrix printers: can withstand harsh
  environments better than laser or inkjet; cheap
  to run and maintain; can use continuous,
  multi-part stationery; very noisy in operation;
  poor print quality; relatively expensive to buy;
  cartridges don't last very long.

● Chapter 3

1 a Data transfer rate is the rate/speed at which
  data is sent from a storage device to a
  computer. Data access time is the time it takes
  to locate the data on the storage device.

b DVD-R allows data to be recorded once
  on the optical media; once data is finalised
  it acts like a DVD-ROM and can only be
  read. DVD-RW allows several read/write
  operations to take place; it requires more
  expensive equipment than DVD-R.

2 a back-up
  b serial access
  c key field
  d direct access
  e transaction file

3 Optical: uses plastic disks coated in light-
  sensitive material or coatings which can be
  converted to pits; surface of disk is read by a
  blue or red laser; disk spins and read/write
  head reads/writes the data as 0s and 1s; uses a
  single spiral track to store data working from
  the centre outwards; devices can be R, R/W
  or ROM.
  Solid state: no moving parts; data retrieved at
  same rate no matter where it is stored; relies on
  the control of the movement of electrons with
  NAND or NOR chips; data stored as 0s and 1s
  in millions of tiny transistors within the chip.

Cambridge IGCSE ICT Study and Revision Guide © Graham Brown and David Watson, 2017

Chapter 4

1 a

Description	Network device
A device that takes a data packet received at one of its input ports and sends the data packet to every computer connected to the LAN.	hub
A device that converts digital data to analogue data (and *vice versa*) to allow the transmission of data across existing telephone lines.	modem
A device that connects a LAN to another LAN that uses the same communication protocols.	bridge
A device that takes a data packet received at one of its input ports and works out its destination address; the data packet is then sent to the correct computer on the LAN only.	switch
A device that enables data to be directed between different networks, for example, join a LAN to a WAN; the main function is to transmit internet and transmission protocols between two networks.	router
A network point (node) that acts as an entrance to another network.	gateway
Hardware which forms part of any device that needs to connect to a network; it often contains the MAC address generated at the manufacturing stage.	NIC

b Set up IP account if internet access required. Purchase necessary hardware and software for the network. Set up system to enable wireless connectivity. Configure all hardware and software on the network. Install common software on server and ensure all network software licences have been purchased. Set up network privileges (for example, network manager). Hardware needed: switch/hub, router, cables, firewalls, servers.

2 a i LAN: local area network; in one building or very close geographically; devices connected by hub or switches.
ii WAN: wide area network; devices connected over a large area geographically (for example, a country); uses existing communications structure (for example, phone lines).
iii WLAN: wireless local area network; same as a LAN but uses wireless connectivity instead of wires; uses WAPs/hot spots as network connection points.

b i

printer queues can cause a big problem	
if the main server breaks down, the whole network goes down	
data transfer rate is much slower	✓
all computers can have access to the same software and files	

ii

medium access card	
media address command	
modem addressing card	
media access control	✓

iii

sender's IP address	
time and date the data packet was sent	✓
identity number of the data packet	
header to identify the data packet	

3 a i heuristic checking
ii false positive
iii hologram
iv digital divide
v authentication
vi Data Protection Act
vii asymmetric
b Prevent illegal/undesirable material being posted on websites as people find it too easy to find information that can have serious consequences; would help prevent children being subjected to undesirable and dangerous websites; stop incorrect/biased information being posted on websites/wikis/blogs; material on the internet is already available elsewhere; expensive to police internet – users would pick up the bill; difficult to enforce rules and regulations globally; freedom of information infringement at risk; laws already exist to deal with illegal material and comments on blogs, and so on.

Chapter 5

1 a Advantages: higher productivity; more consistency; don't take/need breaks; don't go on strike.
Disadvantages: expensive to set up/buy and maintain; can't deal with 'unusual' circumstances; need re-programming for each new task.
b No need to stay at home to cook food or wash clothes/dishes; gives people time for more leisure activities; can use smartphones to control devices away from home; smart

Cambridge IGCSE ICT Study and Revision Guide © Graham Brown and David Watson, 2017

fridges and freezers can lead to a healthier lifestyle; no need to do manual tasks at home.

2 **a** Part-time: staff work fewer than normal hours per week; either fewer hours per day or per month.

Flexi-time: employee can start/finish work at different times to normal workers; however, they must work the full hours per week.

Job sharing: full-time job is divided between two workers who work half of the weekly hours per week; total time worked is the same as a normal worker.

Compressed: employee works full hours for the week but works longer hours than normal per day so completing their hours for the week in fewer days.

b Happier workforce; more likely to remain with the company. Saves money since less training and recruitment required. Possible to extend the hours the company can operate for. Staff avoid rush hour traffic/commute, meaning less stress. Possible for staff to have more time with family/time to do hobbies.

c Built-in obsolescence; expensive to repair/ need specialist staff to repair devices; more complicated operation of device/often have too many features not wanted; hacking issues can lead to problems with the devices.

● Chapter 6

1 **a** Sound sensor and oxygen sensor send data to a data logger. Data is converted to digital and stored. Data collected by personnel on a regular basis or data automatically transmitted back to EA laboratories. Computer in EA laboratory compares new data with old/ stored data. Produces new data, graphs, and so on, showing changes in environment over a given time period and indicates any trends, out-of-range values, and so on. EA scientists would use the data to suggest changes, and so on.

b i infrared sensor

ii Infrared sensor data allows microprocessor to calculate distance between car and vehicle in front; also obtains speed of vehicle and automatically calculates the safe distance between the two vehicles.

iii Sensors send data to microprocessor. Microprocessor uses data to determine if car is at a safe distance. If distance < safe distance it sends a signal to sound a warning buzzer and sends signals to actuators to operate brakes automatically.

2

Application	Suitable sensor
control water content in the soil in a greenhouse	moisture
measure the quality of air in a building	O_2/CO_2
switch on the headlights of a car automatically when it gets dark	light
automatically turn on the wiper blades of a car when it starts to rain	infrared
pick up footsteps of an intruder in a building	acoustic/sound
control the acidity levels in a chemical process	pH

3
```
LEFT 90          FORWARD 40
PENDOWN          RIGHT 45
REPEAT 3         PENDOWN
FORWARD 40       FORWARD 30
RIGHT 90         RIGHT 90
ENDREPEAT        FORWARD 30
LEFT 90          (PENUP)
PENUP
```

4 **a** Robot is programmed with the sequence of instructions. Each instruction copies the action of a human being. Each instruction is tested on a simulation program to ensure correct action. Program then tested on real vehicle and undergoes further modifications if required.

Human operator manually carries out a sequence of instructions. The robot arm is guided by the human operator. Each arm movement is stored as a series of instructions. Once all instructions stored robot arm can do tasks in correct sequence.

Human operator straps sensors to his arm. Actions are then carried out by human operator. Each movement is stored as a set of instructions in computer memory. Sensor sends back data about the arm movements, which are stored in the computer memory.

b Engineers are consulted and key data is collected from them. A knowledge base is designed and the engineer's knowledge collected is used to populate the knowledge base. Rules base is designed and created together with the inference engine. An explanation system is also developed alongside this. The input/output interface is designed. The system is fully tested using data with known outcomes. The system is further modified if test results unsatisfactory.

5 Barcodes on items are scanned by barcode readers at the checkout. If the barcode on the item can't

Cambridge IGCSE ICT Study and Revision Guide © Graham Brown and David Watson, 2017

be read by the scanner, the number under the barcode is keyed in manually. The barcode is searched for on the stock database until a match is found. If no match found, an error message is sent back to the checkout desk. If a match is found, the item price and description is sent back to the checkout. The stock level of the item is read, reduced by 1 and then rewritten back to the item's record on the database. If the stock level of the item <= pre-order level, a check is made to see if a flag has been set to indicate an order has already been made. If no flag has been set, an order for new items is made automatically. When new stock arrives, the stock level database is updated accordingly.

6 a Advantages: driver doesn't need to consult any maps; system can warn of speeding; system can give an estimated time of arrival; it is possible to program in the fastest route or a route avoiding road tolls, and so on; system can give key information such nearest petrol station, and so on.
Disadvantages: if the map is out of date, the GPS can give incorrect instructions; loss of satellite signal can give many problems; incorrect start and end points can give problems.

b

Stage description	Order
brightness and contrast of the number plate are adjusted so it can be read clearly	4
on his return, the driver puts the car park ticket into the machine and pays for his parking	10
sensors detect the car and send signals to the computer	1
each character on the number plate is recognised using OCR software	6
sensors detect the rear of the car and the barrier is automatically dropped	12
each character on the number plate is segmented	5
using OCR software, the characters are converted into a string of editable text	7
an algorithm is used to locate and isolate the number plate from the initial camera image	3
the text string is stored on a database	8
motorist drives to exit barrier and ANPR system recognises number plate and the barrier is automatically raised	11
car park barrier is raised and the driver is issued with a car park ticket	9
computer instructs the digital camera to capture an image of the front of the car	2

● Chapter 7

1 a Observation: this involves watching personnel using the existing system to see how it works; people tend to work in a different way when they know they are being watched – this could skew the results.
Questionnaires: distribution of questionnaires to the workforce, managers or customers to find their views on the current system and how it works; questions are not very flexible and there is no way to clarify a vague or incomplete answer to a question.
Interviews: one-to-one question-and-answer session which is either face-to-face or over the telephone; it is possible to probe more deeply by modifying questions based on previous answers; it is very time consuming and expensive in terms of analyst's time; interviewees cannot be anonymous.

Examine paper documents: the analyst goes through the existing paperwork (for example, operating instructions, accounts, training records) allowing them to decide on memory requirements, input/output devices, and so on; it is a very time-consuming exercise and is therefore, relatively expensive.

b

Item	Analysis	Design
identify suitable hardware and software	✓	
create file structures		✓
produce data flow diagrams	✓	
produce a cost–benefit report	✓	
research current system	✓	
production of algorithms and program flowcharts		✓

c Sample of possible order form:

Online car order form

Name: _____

Dealer: _____ | **Look up address**

Model no.: ⬚⬚⬚⬚⬚⬚⬚⬚⬚ | **Look up model no.**

Colour: ▼ | **Manual** ● | **Automatic** ○

Delivery date: ▼ ▼ ▼

Previous page ◀ | **SUBMIT** | **CLEAR** | ▶ **Options page**

---

2 a
date of birth	length check, character check, range check on dd, mm or yyyy, format check
title	character check
gender	consistency check, character check
order number	format check, length check, look-up check
number of items	range check, character check
email address	look-up check

b i Input password twice and computer software compares the two entries.

ii normal: for example 3, 8, 15
abnormal: for example, –2, 60, TWENTY
extreme: for example 1 or 50

3 Direct: old system stopped overnight and new system introduced immediately. Benefits are immediate and costs are low compared to other methods. Method can be disastrous if it fails.

Parallel: old system and new system run side by side for a time. Provides a back-up if the new system fails. System is relatively expensive and slow since two sets of staff are required to work on the systems.

Pilot: one branch of a company introduces the new system; the other branches use the existing/current system. If the system in the single branch fails, the existing/current system is still available. Still some risk associated with new system and it is slower and more expansive to implement than direct method.

Phased: the new system is introduced part by part; only when each part proves to be successful is the next part introduced. If the system fails, it is possible to go back to the point prior to the failure. It is very time consuming as each part needs to be fully assessed before the next part is introduced

Cambridge IGCSE ICT Study and Revision Guide © Graham Brown and David Watson, 2017

4

Item	User documentation	Technical documentation	Both types of documentation
how to sort and search	✓		
tutorials and FAQs	✓		
sample runs and test results			✓
minimum memory requirements		✓	
hardware/software requirements			✓
how to add/delete/amend records	✓		
systems flowcharts		✓	
meaning of error messages			✓

● Chapter 8

1 a encryption
b cookies
c plain text
d spam
e firewall
f e-safety

2 Spyware:
software that gathers data by monitoring key presses on a user's keyboard; the gathered data is sent back to the person who sent the spyware and gives the originator access to personal data which can lead to fraud, loss of data, and so on; it can also install other spyware and change the user's default web browser
use anti-spyware; use dropdown boxes when entering passwords or use touch screens

Phishing:
creator sends out legitimate-looking emails to target users; as soon as the email is opened and user clicks on a link, they are sent to a fake/ bogus website claiming to be the legitimate company
user is asked to enter personal data leading to fraud, identity theft, loss of money, and so on
many ISPs filter out phishing; don't click on links from emails unless you are 100% certain they are legitimate

Hacking:
act of gathering unauthorised access to a computer
it can lead to identity theft, loss of data, illegal use of personal data, and so on
can minimise the risk using firewalls; use strong passwords and user ids

● Chapter 9

1 a product key
b software piracy
c morality
d ethics
e culture

2 a Age, experience and knowledge of the audience. Language being used; expectations of audience. Use of multi-media and whether it should be interactive. Length of the presentation. Which examples are appropriate for the audience.
b Use of product keys on the software package. The need to sign a licence agreement when loaded up. Use of a hologram on the package.
c The need to supply some of the files on a dongle for each user. Use of the features shown in part b, above. Software features which prevent copying being done.

● Chapter 10

1 a netiquette
b public cloud
c data redundancy
d hits
e active

2 a Public cloud: storage environment where client and provider are different companies. Private cloud: storage provided by dedicated environment behind a firewall; client and provider are integrated as a single entity. Hybrid cloud: this is a mixture of a public and private cloud; sensitive data resides on a private cloud and the remaining data on a public cloud.
b i Rules to be obeyed when posting or transmitting material over a network.
ii No abusive language and messages should be clear. Posts can be read by the public so spelling and grammar should be correct; also privacy should be considered. Don't use capital letters except where necessary and keep emoticons to a minimum.
c Blogs: personal internet journals; one person writes/owns the blog; other people can only read it; entries organised most recent to least recent. Wikis: allow users to create and edit web pages using a web browser; anyone can edit or write a wiki; document history is maintained.

Chapter 11

1 .mp4 and .gif
2 .txt, .rtf and .csv
3 Both file types are containers.
Both file types can hold a number of files with different types.
Both file types contain compressed data …
… and are used to reduce the number of bytes needed to save a file …
… to save storage space/reduce transmission time.
.rar file extension is an acronym for Roshal ARchive; developed by Russian software engineer Eugene Roshal.

Chapter 12

1 Image B   Reflection/rotation through 180 degrees
Image C   Rotation through 90 degrees clockwise
Image D   Cropped
2 Aspect ratio: The ratio of the width to the height of an image.

Chapter 13

1 Author's name; Document title; Chapter title; Company email/address
2 Page numbering; Section numbering; Date of publication; Filename and path

Chapter 14

1 A serif font is a font style where the ends of characters contain small strokes called serifs; if these strokes are not present then it is a sans serif font.
2 Corporate branding/a method of recognising a company through elements like its logo/colour scheme, and so on.
3 To give consistency to documents and other materials.
To save time in planning/setting up/creating/formatting documents.
Creates brand recognition.
Reduces the risk of mistakes in documents.

Chapter 15

1 'marshhland' – Two h's suggest it is not a word, nor the name of a place or object. This is a spelling error.
'Tawara' – This appears to be the name of a place so is unlikely to be held in the dictionary of the spell check program. The capital T also gives us a clue to this, suggesting it is a name.

2 'Mrs jones' should have a capital letter for her name ('Mrs Jones').
The first sentence suggests a female examiner and the second suggests a male examiner. The spell check and grammar check would not identify these errors.

Chapter 16

1 a Pie chart
  b Line graph
  c None of these (it would be a scatter diagram)
  d Line graph

Chapter 17

1 The area between the edge of a page…
… and the main content of the page.
This is usually white space.
Text flows between the page margins.
2 Text which is aligned…
Text which displays straight (not ragged) margins…
… to both left and right margins.
3 The first line of each paragraph is aligned to the left margin.
All other lines are left hanging/indented from the margin.
It is useful for short headings followed by blocks of text.
This is set using hanging indent and first line indent markers on the ruler.
4 One master letter could be created rather than 5450 individual letters …
… reducing the time taken to type the letters
… reducing the number of errors as they are typed.
Different rates for each course only need to be entered once (into the data source) – rather than entered into every letter.
All student data can be taken from existing data files so no need to retype it.

Chapter 18

1 a A record is a collection of fields containing information about one data subject, usually one person or object.
  b A field holds a single item of data.
  c A file is a logically organised collection of records.
  d A table is a two-dimensional grid of data organised by rows and columns within a database.
  e A report is a document that provides information; in a database it is designed to make the data presented easy to understand.
  f A query is a request for information from a database/search to interrogate a database.

Cambridge IGCSE ICT Study and Revision Guide © Graham Brown and David Watson, 2017

g A calculated control is a special field in a database report that is calculated as the report is run.

2 A flat file database contains a single two-dimensional table …
… which holds data about one subject/type of item.
A relational database has more than one table …
… each table holds data about one subject/type of item.
These tables are linked together …
… through common data elements …
… using a system of primary key and foreign key fields.

3 a Price
Descending order
b Tracks
Ascending order
c Released > 2015 AND Price < 10
d Emile Sande, Phil Collins, Michael Buble

● Chapter 19

1 Presenter notes often contain more content than shown on the slides.
Presenter notes can include greater detail than the audience notes.
Presenter notes can contain anecdotes to 'hook' the audience.

2 Continuous looping

● Chapter 20

1 a Looks through the contents of cells H2 to H21.
Checks to see if contents are equal to contents of cell B5.
The contents of the corresponding/matching cells from I2 to I21 are added to the total/summed.
Which gives the value 746.50.
b =SUMIF($H$2:$H$21,B6,$I$2:$I$21)
c =COUNT(I2:I21)

2 When the result of A42*A43 gives a response …
… that has a decimal part of 0.5 or greater …
… then different answers will occur.
The INT function will remove the decimal part.
The ROUND(…,0) function will round up to the next whole number …
… if the decimal part is greater than or equal to 0.5.
Any two suitable examples of data in A42 and A43.

3 a It counts the number of times the contents of cell A3 …

… is stored in the named range ObjectTable …
… which has already been defined by the user.
b $A$3 is an absolute cell reference.
This cell reference will not change when the cell is replicated/copied.
If a relative cell reference like A3 was used, the reference would change when it was replicated/copied.

● Chapter 21

1 a http: hypertext transfer protocol.
Rules that must be obeyed when transferring data over the internet.
b Web browser: this is software that allows a user to display a web page on a computer screen; interprets HTML from a web page. It shows the results as text/images/sound/video.
c ftp: network protocol used when transferring files from one computer to another over the internet.

2 http is used to access the world wide web.
ftp is used to download data from file servers …
… whereas http is used to download data from web servers.
ftp files are transferred from one device to another and then copied into memory.
http transfers the contents of a web page into web browser for viewing.
ftp upload is used for larger files …
… and http is used for smaller files.

3

h1	colour should be color sans serif should be sans-serif 20 px should be 20px (i.e. no space between 20 and px)
h2	000040 should be #000040 Times New Roman should be "Times New Roman" centre should be center
table	"solid" should have no quotes
td	border-colour should be border-color

4 **Content layer**
Is used to create the page structure/layout
Is usually HTML/ uses HTML tags/saved in HTML format
Contains text, images and hyperlinks
Presentation layer
Is used to set display features/parameters of the page
Is usually CSS/saved in CSS format
Presentation layer can be attached as an external stylesheet, set as an internal stylesheet or as embedded tags within the HTML.

Index

It is illegal to photocopy this page